COFFEE SELF-TALK FOR DUDES

5 MINUTES A DAY TO START LIVING YOUR LEGENDARY LIFE

KRISTEN HELMSTETTER

Edited by
GREG HELMSTETTER

Green
Butterfly
Press

Coffee Self-Talk™ for Dudes

Copyright © 2021 by Kristen Helmstetter

ISBN: 978-1-7362735-4-8

v3.0

ABOUT THE AUTHOR

In 2018, Kristen Helmstetter sold everything to travel the world with her husband and daughter. She currently lives in a medieval hilltop town in Umbria, Italy.

She writes romance novels under the pen name Brisa Starr.

You can find her on Instagram:

 instagram.com/coffeeselftalk

OTHER BOOKS BY KRISTEN HELMSTETTER

Coffee Self-Talk: 5 Minutes a Day to Start Living Your Magical Life

Sunday Times Bestseller. This is the original *Coffee Self-Talk*. It's 95% the same book as *Coffee Self-Talk for Dudes*, but oriented toward women.

The Coffee Self-Talk Daily Reader #1

The Coffee Self-Talk Blank Journal (blank with lines)

Coffee Self-Talk for Teen Girls

Coffee Self-Talk for Teen Girls Blank Journal (blank with lines)

The Coffee Self-Talk Guided Journal (coming fall 2021)

CONTENTS

PREFACE

Why "for Dudes"?

In August of 2020, I published the book, *Coffee Self-Talk*, that soon became a bestseller across much of the English-speaking world. The book described a simple process for creating a five-minute morning ritual of speaking to yourself in positive affirmations while drinking your morning coffee (or other beverage). Over time, this simple act reprograms your brain, changing your attitude, beliefs, actions, and ultimately, your life. Many readers even reported feeling a change in their mood or outlook with their very first cup of coffee.

Almost immediately, I began to receive emails from readers telling me their stories about how their daily Coffee Self-Talk ritual had affected their lives. Boosting their spirits during COVID, improving their marriages, giving them the courage to ask for a promotion, or finding a new direction in life.

I also received a lot of questions. One of the most common questions was, "will it work for men?"

Nowhere in *Coffee Self-Talk* did I say that the process was designed for women. It's not. Self-talk will work for anybody... men, women, even kids.

That said, the book was written by a woman (me), with women in mind, as though I were talking to a friend. The examples I provided were from my own life. Many would say the prose was feminine, with words like *shimmer, sparkle, glitter*, and so on. If it was an adjective you might find on a tube of lip gloss, I probably used it in the book.

Also, hearts. Lots of hearts on the cover. Pastel hearts, even. And a picture of girl drinking coffee.

As questions about applying the book to men began to accumulate in my in-box, and feedback about couples doing the program together, it became clear to me that there was a need for this book's information presented in a way that's more oriented for men.

Coffee Self-Talk for Dudes is the result.

This book is perhaps 95% identical to the original *Coffee Self-Talk* book. I have edited certain lines and examples to be more gender-neutral or masculine, or simply more relevant to men.

It wasn't always clear what should be changed. I tried to avoid dumb stereotypes, and besides, some women can get just as excited as men about explosive imagery, power tools, beer, and uber strong muscles... I myself am a former competitive bodybuilder. And men can be moved by natural beauty, sparkling, shiny things, and magic carpet rides.

But just to be safe, I've enlisted the assistance of my husband, who has also edited this book to ensure a proper degree of dude-worthiness.

INTRODUCTION

Dear Reader,

Hi! I'm Kristen, and I'm happy to meet you. I'm in my early 40s, and I recently went through a profound transformation in my life.

I admit, prior to this huge transformation, I already had a pretty cool life. My family (husband, daughter, and myself) all had good health, friends, family, and successes under our belts. I had nothing *real* to complain about. But that didn't stop me from complaining about trivial things. *Champagne problems*, right?

So, we grabbed life by the balls and decided to "sell it all and travel the world."

The first year, we traveled all over Europe. It was exciting and fun, but I realized I was actually running from something—or more precisely, from a lack of something—using travel to escape from a life in which I felt no sense of purpose or direction.

Overall, I had a positive attitude about my life. My cup was usually half-full, but something was missing. My life had no *magic*. Traveling distracted me enough that I could ignore trying to figure out what to do with my life, but it also brought with it a fair amount of stress, as you'd imagine can happen when living in foreign countries, bouncing from one city to another, living out of a suitcase, and constantly moving around. With a child.

Prior to leaving the U.S., I had delved fairly deeply into your run-of-the-mill mindfulness meditation. I had also come to embrace a generally Stoic and Taoist philosophy of seeking balance and "going with the flow," rather than stressing about things that are beyond my control. Both of these helped give me peace, and I was pleased enough with the results. Still, there were too many days when I woke up feeling lost, reluctant to even get out of bed and start my day. Why was this? I was a "quite happy" person, right? I felt blessed and fortunate.

So, why did I still have so many days where I let anxiety and worry grip my heart? For the first six months of our world travels, I relied upon gratitude, meditation, and Taoism to get my ass out of bed. It worked pretty well, but... I lacked gusto. I wasn't shining. I felt all this potential inside me, and I knew, deep down, that I had so much to be happy and grateful for, that I should be kicking ass and flying high like an eagle. But I wasn't.

Readers of my blog (KristenHelmstetter.com) know the rest of the story. After seven months of travel abroad, I had a breakdown. I experienced my dark night of the soul as I grappled with my lack of focus and direction. It was hard and scary, and I felt paralyzed.

However, you can't have a rainbow without the storm, and that breakdown ultimately began a process that resulted in my breakthrough. In that breakthrough, I discovered a new and improved way to live. I also discovered *a process*. A process with results that feel almost miraculous, and that anyone can do.

From that time until this moment as I write this, I've undergone the most amazing transformation. I've found my spirit, my focus, my power, and I now soar like the eagle I knew I could be. I've unleashed my bliss.

There were a handful of techniques that contributed to my epic transformation, which I've previously outlined in my blog. One of the key techniques, or ingredients, to living my legendary life is what I call *"Coffee Self-Talk."* I've discussed it briefly on my blog, but I had a lot more to say about it. So, I wrote the book you're now reading.

It would absolutely rock my world if something in this book jump-starts your transition to living a legendary life. My mom always says, "If you get just one good recipe from a cookbook, it was worth it." When you read this book, my hope is that you'll get one (or ten!) ideas that transform your life. My goal in writing it was to have it help you live a happier, healthier, and epic life. Now is your time to come alive, and today is the start of your happiest life. As you implement the tips and techniques described in this book, you *will* become happier, and you'll become madly passionate about living your life to your ultimate potential.

Come fly with me. You deserve it. We all do!

Love,

Kristen

P.S. In this book, I repeat some points a few times... this is intentional. It will help the concepts stick in your brain, so you'll never forget them. The repetition not only helps you learn, it keeps you motivated to continue.

This is not a one-way conversation. I'd love to hear your story, too. What you tried, and how it's working for you. You can reach me at:

Kristen@KristenHelmstetter.com

Also, write to me to receive a free MP3 recording of the Coffee Self-Talk script, *"Living a Legendary Life."*

I look forward to hearing from you!

PART I

CREATING A LEGENDARY LIFE WITH COFFEE SELF-TALK

Chapter 1

WHAT IS COFFEE SELF-TALK?

Coffee + Self-Talk

Coffee Self-Talk is a powerful, life-changing routine that takes only five minutes per day. It transforms your life by boosting your self-esteem, suffusing you with confidence and happiness, and helping you attract the life you've always wanted. And, very importantly, it creates feelings of wholeness and worthiness. All this, with your next cup of coffee.

Coffee Self-Talk comprises two things: 1) your morning coffee, and 2) your self-talk. If you're not familiar with self-talk, then buckle your seatbelt, because self-talk *will* change your life.

Self-Talk: A Primer

Even if you've never heard of self-talk, you've actually been doing it your whole life. It's been around for a long time, probably since homo sapiens started talking. Here's the short version: Self-talk is simply the words you say and think to yourself. It's your inner voice, your internal dialog. Sometimes it's spoken, sometimes it's silent.

Sometimes you're aware of it, usually you're not... until you are. This book will help you with that.

Self-talk is essentially the dialog you run about yourself, the way you think about you, and the things you do. Your self-talk is the way you see yourself and refer to yourself. Do you think you're smart? Not smart? That's your self-talk. Do you think you're fortunate? Unfortunate? That's your self-talk. Do you think opportunities are all around you? Or nowhere around you? That's your self-talk. Do you think you're handsome? Not handsome? Talented? Not talented? That's all self-talk.

As you can see, self-talk can be good or bad, helpful or harmful. An affirmation (a statement that's said as though it's true) can be positive or negative. Everything we say or think about ourselves, and our lives, *becomes our truth* as we affirm it—positively or negatively. That is, our subconscious believes it, whether it's true or not.

Therefore, we're going to start a process in which we tell our subconscious that the way we want to be is the way things *already are*. The subconscious doesn't judge, it just follows the instructions. It *will* do what you say. It's really that simple, but that doesn't mean it's easy for everyone. Most of us aren't used to being nice to ourselves. That's going to change by the end of this book. You're going to become your own best friend, and when you do, the magic starts, and your epic transformation begins.

While self-talk is ancient, it only started becoming known as "self-talk" in the twentieth century. The idea that people have an inner dialog running in their heads started to be studied in the 1920s. During the '70s and '80s, the term began to enter mainstream awareness, as people realized they could change their brains and their behavior by changing what they say and think to themselves.

As a result, self-talk has become a popular tool in the self-help toolkit, particularly among high-performance individuals such as top executives, entrepreneurs, Olympic athletes, elite military units, and enthusiasts in the life-hacker community. Clinically, self-talk has been used as a cognitive therapy for applications ranging from depression, anxiety, PTSD, addiction, eating disorders, and weight-loss, to cognitive skills, social skills, sales, goal achievement, and academic performance. As of this writing, there are over 9000 citations for "self-talk" in PubMed (the National Institutes of Health's search engine for scientific papers).

Millions of ordinary people have learned about self-talk, too. In the mid-'80s, Dr. Shad Helmstetter wrote a book called *What to Say When You Talk to Your Self*. It would go on to become a self-help classic, selling millions of copies in over 60 languages. Self-talk became widely known as Dr. Helmstetter spent the next thirty years writing more books, speaking all over the world, and giving over a thousand media interviews, including five appearances on the Oprah Winfrey Show.

Even for people who had never heard the term "self-talk," the culture gradually shifted. Imagine the reaction strangers would have today if you scolded your child in public with, *"you'll never amount to anything!"* It sounds so shocking to our modern ears that it's easy to forget that speech like that used to be commonplace. Nowadays, most parents know better. They know that such words can have powerful and lasting harmful effects. Dr. Helmstetter had a lot to do with this cultural paradigm shift.

I had not heard of Dr. Helmstetter when I met his son, Greg, fifteen years ago. (Greg is now my husband. More on that, later.) But I was familiar with the idea that the words you say—both out loud, and in your head—actually matter. A lot. In fact, they matter enough that it's important to choose those words carefully. At least, until you've acquired the habit of saying good stuff and not saying harmful stuff. Eventually, it becomes automatic.

"Coffee Self-Talk" is my own customized, personal version of self-talk. It's a combination of classic self-talk, for boosting self-esteem and adjusting your beliefs and behaviors, plus awesome affirmations, and, if you like, favorite passages from books, song lyrics, quotes, or other words that inspire or uplift you. And, of course, *coffee*. I'm living proof that this combination of words, java, and daily ritual powerfully affect your mood, your behavior, and how you feel about yourself deep down inside. In spite of the conditions in your life right now.

When your self-esteem is boosted, everything in your life changes. You're a rocket blasting into every morning, excited to take on the day. Heck, you're excited for your *life!* When your behaviors—and in particular, your daily habits—are in sync with your long-term goals and dreams, then things in your life seem to magically "happen" for you. Everything clicks.

It turns out, it's *not* magic—it's neuroscience—but it sure feels like magic.

I do my Coffee Self-Talk every day, virtually without fail. It inspires me, and it directs my actions in the direction of my Happy Sexy Millionaire manifestations (more on that later, too). It supercharges every day with power. What could have been a bad day becomes a good day. What starts as a good day becomes amazing. No matter what life has in store, Coffee Self-Talk makes it leagues better. It massively amplifies the good and instantly diminishes the not-so-good. It *will* make all the difference in your world. I promise.

Your daily Coffee Self-Talk advantage is powerful for spinning happiness and confidence into your life, while also bringing you closer to your goals, resolutions, and dream life. It doesn't mean you won't ever have challenges. Rather, it means that life's ordinary challenges won't phase you. Or completely freak you out. It will be like in *The Matrix*, when bullets fly at Neo, and he just bends out of the way, no hits or damage. THAT'S how Coffee Self-Talk works for you when life throws crap your way.

In other words, it's OK when the world tosses you curveballs, because you bob-n-weave some magic, rapidly recovering. That's mastery! That's being the real hero in your life... responding better, stronger, and faster. This gets you back to happiness, in a state of equanimity, and moving forward.

Coffee Self-Talk is life-changing, and I'm excited to be on this journey with you. Later, I'll share examples of my own Coffee Self-Talk and many sample scripts to help get you started. We'll find the perfect time to do it every day—with your morning cup of coffee. And, you'll discover tips and tricks to enhance your self-talk, as though pouring gasoline on it, striking a match, and lighting it... so it explodes with energy, drawing your desires and goals toward you faster than ever. Self-talk, in general, is extremely useful, but *creating a daily program* with self-talk fast-tracks your success and happiness. More on this rad stuff in a bit.

Is Self-Talk Just Positive Thinking?

Self-talk is related in some ways to positive thinking, but it's not actually the same thing.

Positive thinking is important, because you must believe your desired outcomes are possible if you're going to expend effort (or even take risks) to pursue them. Self-talk helps you create new, better beliefs, and it strengthens the ones you want to reinforce. Self-talk therefore helps give you a more positive, constructive view of what is possible. And in particular, of what you're capable of accomplishing.

Skeptics often dismiss "positive thinking" as unrealistic or wishful thinking. This is sometimes correct, such as when someone fails to assess the risks associated with taking some course of action. But the space between what people think they can do, and what they are *actually capable* of doing, is VAST. We could all stand to take a few more risks. It's human nature to be risk averse—fearing the downside more than striving for the upside. In fact, many perceived risks are actually based on fears that are completely made-up. Phantoms and bogeymen from beliefs we've held since childhood, such as fear of failure, or fear of what others may think about us.

For most people, positive thinking is a correction toward a much more accurate assessment of what is truly possible.

Positive thinking can also cause problems when it makes people pretend that real problems don't exist. Problems do exist, of course. Or assuming the problems will go away without taking any action. Self-talk, done properly, has nothing to do with wishing away problems. Quite the opposite... self-talk is *proactive*. It equips you to see things in new ways and gives you the power to take action to solve problems. And, in many cases, to prevent problems in the first place!

Isn't Self-Love Just Narcissism?

No. In fact, it's almost the exact opposite. *Narcissism* is excessive admiration of oneself. The key word being *excessive*. In its extreme version, pathological narcissism is a personality disorder characterized by severe selfishness, lack of empathy, a sense of entitlement, a need for admiration, and the belief that the individual is better, smarter, and more deserving than everyone else.

But here's the thing... narcissism is *always* the result of a *deep sense of self-loathing*, in which the ego protects itself by artificially propping itself up, to absurd degrees, and to the detriment of everyone else.

Truly confident people don't brag; they feel no need to. Nor do they crave attention. Or feel the need to always be "right." Whenever you see somebody who seems otherwise confident exhibiting these traits, what you're actually witnessing is a frightened ego seeking external validation.

In short, narcissism is based on fear.

Self-love is the opposite.

Many positive self-talk affirmations (and the Coffee Self-Talk scripts in this book) build upon the concept of self-love, which becomes the rock-solid foundation upon which lasting, positive change is possible.

Without self-love, it is very difficult for people to see themselves as *worthy...* of receiving what they desire. And they will often unconsciously self-sabotage their efforts, such as by failing to follow through.

For this reason, the Coffee Self-Talk scripts in this book contain many *self-love* and *self-affirming* affirmations, such as:

I'm a powerful and creative genius.

I am brave.

I love me.

I am magnificent. I am a magician.

I am strong, virile, and mighty.

And so on.

Lines like these are designed very specifically to program your brain with self-belief. They are your *self*-talk... not what you go around telling the world, unless your intention is to teach others how to do it, or to spread the idea of healthy self-esteem, or set an example, such as to friends and loved ones. They are not boasts. They are never meant to be used to try to impress others.

Once you have programmed your brain to believe, *and feel,* thoughts such as these, they will become internalized and manifest in all kinds of ways, some of which will be apparent to the world, and many of which will not, because it will be your own internal, relaxed, happy, powerful state-of mind. Which is the furthest thing possible from the internal state of a narcissist.

And speaking of spreading the idea, when my family was hunkering down with my mom in the U.S. for six months after COVID-19 broke out, I wanted to continue doing my self-love and self-talk habits, even though we were visitors in someone else's home. One of my favorite things is to write a handful of my Coffee Self-Talk lines on Post-it Notes, one affirmation per note. I wrote about 20 of them and stuck

3–4 on the bathroom mirror, and then rotated them with new ones every few days.

We shared the bathroom with my mom, so I told her what I was doing with the sticky notes. She probably thought it was weird, but I explained how important my self-talk was, and how it was instrumental in my success and happiness. And she was very supportive, as always. But secretly, I knew that having those notes on the mirror would mean she would read them, too!

I also wouldn't have cared if visitors saw them, though we had no visitors due to the lockdown. In fact, I would've loved it. The notes on the mirror create an opportunity to share something that changed my life and could change their lives, too. Loving ourselves, whether public or private, is a good thing when it comes from the heart.

And guess what! My mom even created a few self-talk Post-it Notes of her own and stuck them to the mirror, right next to mine!

Instructional vs. Motivational Self-Talk

Self-talk comes in two flavors. The first is *instructional* self-talk, which involves a list of instructions. It's commonly used by athletes and performers. For example, as a golfer addresses the ball, he might run through a list of instructions and inner commentary to improve his performance. Many basketball players go through a little self-talk routine when preparing to shoot a free throw. Actors similarly prep themselves before going on stage.

Self-talk is incredibly effective for athletes and performers because it helps with technique, focus, and execution. The words initiate a whole cascade of neural and physiological patterns that have been drilled and drilled, in countless hours of practice. It helps them get into "the zone," or "flow." This form of self-talk also helps people focus on the present moment, and not be distracted by past errors or fears of making mistakes.

The second form of self-talk, which is the focus of this book, is *motivational* self-talk. This form boosts self-esteem, increases drive and effort, and creates your optimal, ideal mindset. As a result, it helps you attain your life's dreams while simultaneously feeling like an unstoppable badass on that journey. More specifically, motivational self-talk helps you attain your goals, whether personal or professional, small or huge. It can help you heal your body and become healthier. It can be used to boost your finances or find the mate of your dreams. There is no limit to the ways that self-talk can improve your life.

In this book, I'll show you how to create your own mega-empowering Coffee Self-Talk script that you'll use to create and live your BEST, *most legendary* life.

All Self-Talk—Positive or Negative—Impacts You NOW

I mentioned that self-talk goes both ways. It can be either good or bad. So be mindful of your self-talk because it's extremely powerful. The words you think and say to yourself, good or bad, *will* create that life for you. You have the power to choose that life, right in your very own brain and mouth. Good self-talk is the foundation of a good life. Bad self-talk is a surefire recipe for a crappy life. It's that simple.

How do you know when self-talk is bad? It's easy... bad self-talk is any word or thought about you, your life, your circumstances, or the world that isn't uplifting. If you complain or criticize anything or anyone, it's bad self-talk. Don't like the size of your biceps? That's bad self-talk. Not happy with your car and complaining about it? That's poor self-talk. Feel like you don't deserve a raise? That's really shitty self-talk. Feel like you aren't good enough to deserve the love of someone wonderful? That's totally fucked-up self-talk.

Good self-talk is like having a tornado of awesome thoughts that feel good swirling around your brain and flying out of your mouth. You feel uplifted and energized as they ignite power, confidence, and joy when thought or uttered. When you congratulate yourself on a job well done, or you think you look attractive no matter what, or tell yourself you have the skill or courage to go after what you want—these are all examples of good self-talk. Any words that fill your cup, make you feel inspired, worthy, and whole... those are awesome self-talk.

Now that you're aware of the difference, you must accept the responsibility that all of your self-talk—good or bad—is a *choice*. Your choice. You *choose* to use good self-talk or bad self-talk.

Which will you choose?

Now you know the secret. The key lies within your brain. You have the power. You can use it any way you want.

> *Give life to your dreams, give strength to your visions, and give light to your path.*
>
> — SHAD HELMSTETTER

The question for you and me, and for all of us... is how will you use this power you now know you have? Contemplate this for a moment. Close your eyes and feel it.

It sounds simple—"I'm gonna do GOOD self-talk from now on!"—but that doesn't mean it's easy for everyone. We'll get there though, no worries. Saying nice things to yourself, about yourself, can be a difficult adjustment for some, especially anybody with low self-esteem. The words can feel literally hard to say, because they are too incongruous with that person's self-image.

But I promise, once you get started, it gets really easy. *And cool, too!*

Take a moment and think back to the last time you looked in the mirror. What did you think (or say) to yourself? When you dressed and brushed your teeth this morning, did you feel love toward yourself? Were you happy with your physique? If so, that's great—high five! Keep it up, because that creates a day full of excitement and opportunity. You're going to jump into Coffee Self-Talk with both feet, no problem.

However, maybe it wasn't that rosy. Was your self-talk negative? Did you criticize yourself? If so, you're creating negative energy that follows you throughout your day, like Pig-Pen's swirling cloud of dirt and bugs.

Don't worry, it's OK. Well, it's not OK... it's *normal*... but what I mean is, don't worry, we'll fix that shit. Coffee Self-Talk to the rescue! Self-talk can be used to create a whole new you, a new personality, and that's exciting news!

Or heck, maybe you ignored yourself and zoned out, trimming your beard on autopilot. Neutral perhaps, but a missed opportunity, nonetheless.

How to Have Awesome Self-Talk

Good news! Good self-talk is simply choosing good, positive, uplifting thoughts—as often as possible. Your self-talk is powerful! It's a brilliant tool that will bring more abundance into your life. All it takes is practice, and using this Coffee Self-Talk program is an easy way to do it. Change your self-talk, and you change your life.

If you want amazing health, use healthy self-talk. If you want to make more money, use prosperous self-talk. If you want more confidence, use empowering self-talk. Whatever you want to improve or change, self-talk will accelerate your changes tenfold.

It all starts with your words, thoughts, feelings, and language... your self-talk. Making more money comes with feeling worthy. If you don't truly feel worthy—deep down—you can fix this entirely with self-talk. Becoming super healthy comes from feeling whole. Feeling whole can be programmed with words you say about your mind, body, health, and habits. Everything starts with your self-talk. It's not only the starting point, but also the biggest driver for accomplishing your goals.

Fixing your self-talk can be as simple as thinking to yourself something like, "I'm really productive and good at writing." Or, when someone says, "Hi, how are you doing?" You reply with a big response like, "I'm super!" or "I'm incredible!"

This might feel weird at first. Over the top, silly, dorky, and strange. But it's not! The more times you do it, I swear, the more fun it gets, especially when you watch people's reactions. I love it when someone asks me how I'm doing, and they're expecting the typical, "I'm fine," but then I blast them with an *"I'm incredible!"* Or even... *"I'm freakin' fantastic!"* It's funny when they do a double-take. After the brief shock wears off, they can't help but reply with a bit of awe, "Wow. Um, that's cool."

After any strangeness wears off, these positive replies become your new comfortable norm. And then, if you don't respond with something big and positive, you actually won't feel quite right, like something is missing. But during the initial phase, when positive affirmations still sound strange coming out of your mouth, the thing you need to realize is that *you don't really have to believe the words at first.* Over time, you will! That's the power of self-talk.

You'll rewire your brain—it happens automatically, just by saying the words. It's how we're all designed. In fact, the way you feel today—good or bad—is the result of brain-programming words that you've received in the past, from parents, teachers, friends, television, social media, etc. And, in particular, words you've thought or said to yourself.

When you say, "I am... healthy, great, powerful, confident, etc...." you command your mind to move toward a certain experience. Your life starts to go in that direction, driving you toward a new destiny—one of your own design. ("Destiny" literally means *destination.*) It's very easy. We'll soon get into the details of how to write your own self-talk, and why to combine it with coffee.

Adjusting your self-talk rewrites your current programs, tuning your brain's instrument panel to direct your behavior and actions to start living the way you were really meant to live. If you've had bad self-talk up until now, no worries. Anyone can start fixing it right now. You have the power. Today, this very second.

This book is a tool, and your commitment to the easy program outlined within these pages will determine your success. Remember, you're free *in every moment* to think life-uplifting and powerful thoughts... or not. You can choose. Every choice is a chance to make change.

Sooooo... How Is Your Self-Talk These Days?

I was pretty shocked when I took some time to listen to my own self-talk. It was a profound moment for me. I'd thought I had good enough self-talk, but ohhh noooo, I wasn't even close. My self-talk actually kinda sucked.

When I realized everything we say is an affirmation of some type, that it's either a positive or a negative affirmation, and that it creates our reality, I took a hard look at the words I was saying to myself every day. Each word, every thought.

Even though I thought a lot of positive things about myself, I was jolted to discover that I actually thought many more negative things. I was a harsh critic of myself, and I counted far more negative comments and thoughts about myself, and the world in general. It could be about anything... a gray hair, wrinkles, frumpy-looking clothes, food I was eating, finances, energy levels, my circumstances, people around me, etc.

Despite being a generally positive person (or so I thought), I sure managed to find an awful lot to complain about. Even if these were micro-complaints, they slowly chipped away at my self-esteem, health, and life experience. But I didn't know that! Here's where it can be sneaky. You see, I had enough good self-talk going on in my life that my bad self-talk wasn't completely detrimental. On the whole, my self-talk was "good enough"—and therefore, I didn't realize I was saying anything negative. I didn't realize how much better things could be.

For example, let's say my self-talk on a typical day comprised 37 negative and 63 positive instances. The positives dominated, making me feel more positive than negative, so my self-talk wasn't negative enough to make me feel the need for change. But just one of those negative points affects my brain negatively, in the short term and long term. *Just one!* I didn't realize that *every* negative thought shuts you down, even if just a bit. These add up and lead to sucky consequences. Opportunities vanish, like the light when the power goes out on the grid. Or like a magician's trick, here and then gone—*poof!* Negative self-talk really is that powerful, and it's not how you want to live. It's not how you *were meant* to live.

This was eye-opening for me. This moment of self-reflection, this insight, was a briefly tender and sad moment, too, as I realized how I'd been treating myself badly for so many years. I actually mourned for a bit, knowing I'd been cloaking my life in unnecessary and damaging darkness. *But...* it was also super encouraging, because there was so much room for improvement.

There were now tons of opportunities to uplift myself. This insight lit a burning fire in my core, and I fully embraced how my life was going to change, once I cut out the negative shit-talk and replaced it ALL with positive words. And I mean ALL! The challenge, though, can be making that complete change. Because the truth is, we don't need *any* negative self-talk. Nada. Zilch. Each instance, no matter how small, has a price. It's death from a thousand cuts; it doesn't slay you in a single negative instance or thought, but you slowly die a little more with each harmful utterance.

You see, your self-talk is not only important for your self-esteem, but it also takes root in every facet of your life, including a dramatic impact on your health. When you have positive self-talk all the time, it's like a super-protective, nutrient-dense vitamin infusing your body with golden healing essence. It's not mystical either, though the words I use to describe it might seem so.

Good self-talk makes you feel better, and when you feel better, your endocrine system secretes lower levels of stress hormones. This is beneficial because, over time, the effects of chronic stress literally kill you. And when you experience less stress, your body heals faster! To put it poetically, your loving self-talk creates the potent environment that bathes your cells in the powerful elixirs of manifestation. Envision *that* glory!

Step Up to the Plate: Take Responsibility Today for Your Life

You have tremendous opportunity when you're less dependent on the conditions in your outer world, or when you're subject to the choices other people make. Your self-talk is important because what you think about yourself becomes your "truth." Your truth becomes your life, your destiny. In fact, how you feel about yourself is the driving force behind whether you have a good day, a ho-hum day, or a crappy day. Think about it... how you feel right now is the result of how you thought about yourself this morning, yesterday, last week, and last month.

We have to make this change ourselves, each and every one of us. Your life isn't going to improve unless you make it happen. The good news is that everything you need is within you. Right here and right now; it's all up to you. You will find your own wellspring—or geyser! —of happiness and success, from directly inside yourself. It's just that most of us didn't know we were capable of such power.

Sound too good to be true? It's not! It's the way we were meant to live. Imagine you're standing in front of a door. It's closed right now. On one side is your amazing life, filled with thrills, love, confidence, excitement, shooting stars, and your dreams coming true. On the other side is YOU. You stand there, hand on the knob. All it takes to open that door is for you to think "door-opening" thoughts. It's a Jedi-like power. You say the right positive, uplifting things about you and your life. The door's handle turns golden and shimmers with warmth and shines from the energy you transfer to it. You feel uplifted with these thoughts you're now telling yourself, and the handle turns. So easily, too. You open the door and walk through it, to everything you always knew you could be. It's all you, and it was always there, just waiting for you to take the first step.

Life is from the inside out. When you shift on the inside, life shifts on the outside.

— KAMAL RAVIKANT

Chapter 2

COFFEE SELF-TALK

How to Do Coffee Self-Talk (the Short Version)

The steps are easy:

1. Make yourself a cup of coffee every day (or tea, or water... whatever is your thing).
2. While you sit down to drink it, spend the time savoring the coffee—really *taste* it—while filling your brain with powerful affirmations (words you say to yourself) at the same time.
3. For greater results, speak them out loud.

And that's it.

The following phrases are samples of my personal Coffee Self-Talk (taken from Chapter 5):

*I love life. I love my life. **I love me!***

I bless everything in my life right now. My coffee, my chair, my bed, my family, my friends, my whole life.

I am an amazing person because I am kind and generous.

Life is full of opportunities everywhere I turn. I'm going for it!

I love today because I'm in charge of my day. I make it what I want! I feel powerful.

I am uplifted, in this very moment, because I take care of **me**. *I deserve this time to prepare my day and make it the best day ever.*

I'm having an awesome day today! I smile brightly, I am excited about everything that will happen today, hour by hour.

I'm a magnet for success, prosperity, abundance, and everything I desire.

I let go of all fear, right now. I'm taking responsibility for my success, now, and for the rest of my life. I'm on a mission.

I LOVE feeling so awesome! Yesssssssss!!!

These thoughts and feelings instruct your brain and body, like a blueprint, so you make better choices, make fewer mistakes, feel stronger emotionally, and love your life more than you ever thought possible.

You'll feel some results instantly! You might also feel some resistance, or strange saying it, initially. Either way, you'll find that, as you continue saying your new self-talk, you will change over the next 2–3 weeks. I'm talking *dramatic* change. As in, becoming a new person. Brilliant metamorphosis shit. Your brain literally begins to rewire itself when you do self-talk. (More on that later.)

Why Coffee?

Traditional self-talk instructions make no mention of sipping delicious, hot, caffeinated beverages. (Or, again, whatever your beverage of choice is. From here on, every time I say *coffee*, just replace it with your preferred drink.)

Anchoring the process to your morning coffee has the following benefits:

1. Ritualization

When you ritualize a behavior, you give it special meaning. This meaning gives it more importance, which makes you take it more seriously. The more ceremonial, the better. And because rituals are repeated, they become partly automated, which is the key to establishing something as habit. (For more on habits, see Chapter 13.)

2. Consistency

It's not like you're ever going to forget your morning coffee. Ninety percent of success in life is just sticking with something long enough for it to work. Whether it's exercise, a diet, a financial plan, or career advancement, persistence is the name of the game. When you link self-talk to a part of your daily routine that you're very unlikely to skip, then just imagine the long-term, compounding benefits to your well-being and success.

3. Multi-Sensory Modalities

Linking your ritualized self-talk to the act of drinking coffee will connect the words you say to the sensory and physiological experience of drinking a warm, delicious beverage. If your beverage of choice has caffeine, then you get the added benefit of ingesting a nootropic stimulant as you say your affirmations. This means the brain pays more attention to what you're saying. Not to mention, all future coffee becomes an instant "state dependent" trigger of your most empowered, resourceful mental state, just like how Pavlov's dogs slobbered whenever he rang the dinner bell.

4. Joy

Because, let's face it, coffee is f*cking delicious.

Why Will You Start to Love Your Life by Doing Coffee Self-Talk?

Because when you change your thoughts, you change your brain, you change your focus, and you change your reality. With new positive thoughts, you have new choices, and these choices give you new behaviors. Once your behaviors change for the better, you have new experiences and new feelings. *Bam!*... welcome to a whole new you!

Combining my coffee with my daily self-talk is one of the tools I used to bring about huge changes in my life. By doing my Coffee Self-Talk, I empower myself to take action and realize my dreams, with a fresh, new perspective every day, from the moment I start the morning with my coffee.

Think about coffee in that way for a moment... a mysterious, magical elixir giving you the superpower of total self-belief! I know... it sounds a little silly, but bear with me. It only sounds silly because coffee doesn't actually do that by itself. But self-talk does!

When you combine the two, you link them together in your brain. By drinking coffee while you do your self-talk, and repeating this ritual every day, you anchor the *benefits* of self-talk to the *experience* of drinking coffee.

Did you know that rats who are irradiated (and made sick) after eating a uniquely flavored food will get sick in the future when they taste the same flavor, even when no radiation is administered? The brain does crazy stuff like that, all the time! It makes things real!

With Coffee Self-Talk, you're using this weird quirk of our brains to summon, on demand, your most empowered mental state. Every morning! Or multiple times a day!

It also makes you feel great, right now. There's no waiting. It's immediate. When you do your Coffee Self-Talk, everything is uplifted, in the exact moment of doing it. So, while there are definitely some delayed benefits to self-talk (like attracting abundance into your life overall), you'll also feel more happiness with the very first words of your self-talk, every time. It's simply what your brain does. It also instantly boosts your energy (well, that and the caffeine—haha), and you set up your day for superstar success.

Put another way, if you're feeling crappy, down, or your soul is lethargic, it's impossible to stay at that low-level of living when you're uttering your self-talk. I'm not saying you'll go from zero to 10 in your attitude every time (though that's how it now works for me and many others), but it will shift in an upward direction. And an object in motion tends to stay in motion.

It's simply impossible to stay in total darkness when you're reading or saying uplifting things. Any improvement is helpful; going from zero to three, or even from zero to one. It's a shift for the better. It will make a difference every time. Over time, that difference can be as distinct as flipping on a light switch—going from zero to 10 instantly —in just one session of Coffee Self-Talk, because you'll have trained your brain to do so.

How Did Coffee Self-Talk Start?

In my early twenties, I started playing around with self-talk, in my own way. I'd practice motivational conversations in the mirror with myself, always choosing feel-good words and thoughts. But at the time, I didn't realize that what I was doing was called "self-talk."

In golf, I would also address the ball with instructional self-talk, going through a checklist, and giving myself a little mental pre-swing high-five. I was particularly fond of using self-talk before job interviews, too. It was effective in boosting my self-esteem and helping me display the kind of confidence that only comes from someone who's genuinely relaxed.

So, I was no stranger to self-talk. But it wasn't until I met my husband that I learned "self-talk" was actually a thing. How could I not know this term? I was a full-on Tony Robbins fan, a self-help devotee. And how did my handsome date (now my husband) know about this interesting thing called self-talk? We were definitely destined to be together.

Turns out, his dad, Shad Helmstetter, now my father-in-law, is considered by many to be *the father of self-talk,* for doing perhaps more than anyone in history to popularize the concept. So, yeah, my husband knew a thing or two about it.

As a person who enjoyed hanging out in the self-help section of the bookstore, I considered myself as having a positive outlook on most things in life. If I encountered a challenge or problem, I assumed that a solution existed somewhere, even if I didn't know what it was yet. I was a believer that time healed all wounds. That people are basically good, that dark clouds have silver linings, that setbacks make me stronger, and so on.

But I didn't follow a self-talk program, per se. I just knew it was better to think good thoughts than bad thoughts. But because I wasn't intentional or structured with my approach, such as having a program, it took me longer to bounce back from falls, challenges, and failures. My generally good attitude ensured I would *eventually* rebound, but —oh my goodness—it could have been SO much faster. And I could've prevented so many falls in the first place, if my perspective had been properly tuned. Knowing what I know now, life is magnitudes better with a self-talk habit. Life is just plain *easier.*

And that's what self-talk promises. If you regularly use self-talk—and the key to doing it regularly is to make it a habit (*ahem...* a daily habit, with your cup of coffee), then you can live an incredible life and feel amazing, almost all the time. Your brain rewires for awesomeness, and you become a new you.

That's the trick: finding the time to do it, and regularly. I mean, let's be honest, you can find a thousand times a day to talk to yourself positively. While walking to the kitchen from the bedroom, while peeing or brushing your teeth, while driving your car, while mowing the lawn—these are all opportunities to tap into your inner voice and be uplifted.

However, by doing self-talk while drinking your morning coffee, you never miss a day. It becomes a great habit, with absolute regularity, because no self-respecting coffee drinker skips their coffee! By connecting the two activities of drinking coffee and doing your self-talk, it becomes *automatic*.

There's more to it though. When I'm doing my Coffee Self-Talk, I'm not just sitting there thinking positive things between slurps, entertaining the first fluffy rainbow cloud that comes to my mind. *Ohhh noooo*, it's much more deliberate. I've designed a whole program and dialed it in for easy implementation and uber success.

> *Consistent positive self-talk is unquestionably one of the greatest gifts to one's subconscious mind.*
>
> — EDMOND MBIAKA

Coffee Self-Talk at Its Most Basic Level

1. Get pen and paper, a journal, your computer, or your smart phone with an app like Evernote or Notes. (I use the Notes app on my iPhone.)
2. Write 15 to 20 great things about yourself. Use first person and present tense. For instance, *I am a happy, sexy, millionaire.* (I say this even though I'm not a literal millionaire yet. This speaking of the future as though it's the present is *very* important.) These 15 to 20 phrases are your self-talk, and they can include your own kick-ass positive affirmations, lyrics from songs that light you up, inspiring quotes that you can change into first person, etc. You'll use them every day, and you're free to make changes all the time.
3. Wake up, get your delicious cup of coffee, and sip it while reading your self-talk, over and over. Rinse and repeat, until you've finished drinking your coffee. Reading out loud is best, if possible, even if you're whispering it. Do this every morning with your coffee, making it your Coffee Self-Talk.

4. Enjoy the awesome day YOU just created.

This is really just scratching the surface. Keep reading to learn why this is so powerful, and how to create your own super *badass* Coffee Self-Talk program.

Coffee Self-Talk "Habit Stacking"

One day while I was listening to James Clear's audiobook, *Atomic Habits*, I realized what I was actually doing with my Coffee Self-Talk was my own version of what he calls "habit stacking." Habit stacking is one of the reasons Coffee Self-Talk is so effective. You're taking one positive habit, self-talk, and stacking it on top of another habit you already love doing, drinking coffee. This uses your time efficiently and creates a connection you can use to your advantage.

In my case, I was already going to drink coffee, which I love, and by adding self-talk to it, it's relatively effortless to create a mega power-house self-talk habit that persists over time. If I had tried to do this without the coffee... well, who knows if it would've stuck. Maybe, maybe not. As it turned out, my daily cup of coffee is filled with brilliant affirmations that shape my day. Oddly enough, I now actually enjoy my coffee more than I did before! So power up by tying together an old, attractive habit with a new behavior you'd like to become a habit. That's habit stacking.

The great thing is, you have time for this program. You're already drinking a cup of coffee. Now you're being smarter with your time and giving it more purpose. Intentionality. Instead of wasting time checking social media or skimming email, do something guaranteed to increase your happiness and personal effectiveness in just a few minutes.

Doing the old stuff, like social media, reinforces *the old you*. We're interested in *transformation*. Because we want to live epic lives of abundance and happiness, we're learning new habits, like Coffee

Self-Talk, for *our new selves*. So instead of doing things first thing in the morning that fall under the label of *consumption*, level-up by immediately stepping into your own power with positive self-talk. Become a *creator* with your self-talk first thing in the morning, and watch how fast your life changes.

It's important to understand a thing or two about making habits stick. To start, when you want to form a new habit, it helps if you *believe* it's a desirable habit, and that you feel good about it. Not just because other people say the habit is good, but because you believe it yourself. Giving it a positive meaning, and knowing it benefits you, aligns your will with your purpose. When this happens, resistance evaporates, quickening the process to reach your success.

Now, to make good habits stick, you want to make a plan for when and where to do the behavior that will become the habit. With a plan, you're more likely to follow through. Coffee Self-Talk is exactly this sort of plan! We love our coffee, and now we're anchoring it to a new habit we'd like to create, self-talk. It becomes a self-reinforcing loop, and your new, amazing identity will reinforce your brilliant self-talk habit, for lifelong change.

Not only do we have this new habit in the morning, but because it's anchored with the aroma and taste of coffee, it won't be long before our minds turn to positive self-talk at other times in the day. For example, when you drink a second cup later in the morning or early afternoon, your mind can't help but wander into positive self-talk territory. Heck, just walking by a coffee shop roasting or brewing coffee can trigger your positive self-talk! The first time this happens to you, you'll chuckle with a knowing nod.

Change your thoughts, and you change your world.

— Norman Vincent Peale

Chapter 3

THE INCREDIBLE BENEFITS OF COFFEE SELF-TALK

First things first! Anyone can use self-talk and benefit from the profound results and resilience it offers. Men, women, children, teenagers, or seniors... we can all begin reaping the benefits instantly. You just have to start, and make the commitment to do it every day, which you'll discover is easy to do. Once you begin, you'll see that self-talk *is as addictive as your coffee.*

Benefit #1: Coffee Self-Talk to Live Your Legendary Life!

As you're now discovering, Coffee Self-Talk is a powerful program because it allows you to create a new self-identity with a simple, life-shaping stream of positive affirmations of your own choosing. On the surface, the affirmations might seem like they're just words, but their effect on you goes much deeper. This powerful inner conversation of yours fixes, shapes, and reprograms your subconscious, and actually changes you into a dynamic new person. This is where you come alive, because it primes your brain and body, filling you with feel-good neurotransmitters and endorphins.

That is, it not only makes you more effective and good at attracting possibilities, but it also makes you happier in the moment.

As a result, Coffee Self-Talk *massively* amps up your life with blazing energy and enthusiasm. You'll discover that the phrases and bold words spark lightning in you the moment they leave your mouth. They'll make you strong, like the brilliant star you are. Lit from within like this, you'll feel better... blissful, in fact. Even euphoric. This, in turn, attracts a more extraordinary life to you, because you become a magnet for everything amazing. Your life becomes easier because it flows effortlessly.

Once you start, you'll know exactly what I'm talking about. Things will start to change, some small and some huge. You'll soon find yourself easier-going, less judgmental, and just way friggin' happier. That's how it begins for all of us.

And then, you get on a roll, and so many crazy-cool synchronicities start happening, you can't help but pinch yourself. After a while, it becomes par for the course. Your life shifts to epic greatness because it's now the new normal, and you begin to expect it.

It will feel mystical, but it's just science. The words you choose to think and say will program your behavior in specific ways. The phrases you select will trigger particular feelings and emotions caused by the chemicals your own body releases in response. These uplifted emotions we've created from our Coffee Self-Talk help us make endorphins (opiate peptides) and the so-called "feel-good" neurotransmitters, such as dopamine, serotonin (the "happiness" hormone), and oxytocin (the "love and bonding" hormone). In fact, scientists keep finding more of these, such as the neurotransmitter anandamide, which is known as the "bliss molecule." Our brains make it when we're in elevated emotional states. That's cool!

With your self-talk, you'll choose the words you say, in order to fit your situation and maximize the impact. These words are not only key for feeling amazing in any moment (the short-term benefit), but they're also the source of the *magicky* science that'll make your long-term goals and dreams come true.

Suffice it to say, you'll feel so much damn better, healthier, stronger, and happy with Coffee Self-Talk. You'll find more favorable opportunities, meaningful relationships, and fun times around every corner. You'll find that your whole view of the world changes. The blinders come off, and unique possibilities you weren't previously aware of suddenly appear before you. The truth is that these opportunities were always there, but your selective attention filtered them out, based on your former mental state and beliefs about the world.

You'll find yourself able to do things you never thought possible. In fact, Coffee Self-Talk is a big part of how I became an author of romance novels, when I never thought it was possible.

Benefit #2: Loving Yourself, Finally

When you look at yourself in the mirror, straight into your eyes, how do you feel about that person you're looking at? Do you respect him? Is he living up to your standards? Your expectations? Is he shaping up to be the kind of man you hoped you would become?

If you answered yes to these questions, that's fantastic!

If not, you're not alone. Self-love and self-respect are always in short supply... our culture seems in many ways to be designed to make us feel inadequate.

And that's a problem. Because if you don't first figure out how to love yourself, it's going to be very difficult to succeed at anything else, because deep down, you won't feel like you deserve to be happy.

Self-talk is the answer. It naturally includes thinking and saying loving things to yourself, and you respond with kindness towards yourself through your thoughts and actions.

For example, consider someone who isn't happy about his physical condition. But he starts affirming appreciation for himself and his body, nonetheless. This isn't his usual sentiment. Previously, he would complain and sigh, or look away, whenever he saw his body in the mirror. But now, he has decided to start thinking and saying better things to himself—he is determined to kick ass and feel good about himself, to confidently appreciate himself, all with a new way of talking to himself.

After a few days of sticking with this new "I'm a rock star" routine, he starts to notice a shift. He finds himself being nicer to himself, more appreciative and easygoing, criticizing himself less. After another week, he actually starts to think he's better looking than he's ever been. His appreciation toward himself, spoken consistently, has begun to reverberate back, such that he now actually begins to see himself in a radical, new, awesome light.

The really crazy part—the *magical* part—is that he actually *is* more handsome now... literally more attractive to other people. Humans are finely attuned, often subconsciously, to the subtlest of changes in physical presence: facial expressions, posture, poise, mannerisms, speech, confidence, and so on. When energized, groovy and confident vibes start to flow from you, *people notice!*

For some people, it will be a bit slow-going at first. Saying the words might seem insincere, and that's OK. Keep up the effort. It *will* work. You *will* change. More self-love will flow through you, and from you.

Second, using your Coffee Self-Talk to feel a deep love for yourself makes your dreams easier to attain because you start to really believe in yourself. It makes your life easier to live because you're not as stressed, and you're resilient. Not to mention, you're more fun to be around. Don't underestimate the power your self-love has for making your dreams come true.

The key point is that it's important to love yourself as you are, *now*, while directing your brain to the new you that you're becoming. For example, you don't wait to love yourself once you lose the weight you don't like or build the muscles you want. Rather, you love yourself *as you are now,* and then watch as the weight effortlessly sheds, or your workouts take on a new intensity, as a result of having the new self-identity of a fit and super sexy man. Strut yo' stuff! Now!

Why does this work? It's simple. When you love yourself as you are now, you make choices to support that love of your body. And those choices are effortless; they're not stressful or whiney. For instance, by loving your body now, maybe you choose healthier foods, or smaller portions, *without even realizing it...* your subconscious does all the heavy lifting. A person who loves his body doesn't regularly abuse it. When your self-talk changes, your behavior changes. Or, think about this... maybe you opt for that slice of chocolate cake, because, yes, you love yourself, and you're going to enjoy it. You'll love yourself the whole time you're eating it, with each bite, savoring, and there is *no guilt.* That is powerful, too!

The first example is obvious; you chose healthy food, and it helped make you healthier. The second example—the decadent cake—is less obvious. It means having so much joy and love for yourself, there are no thoughts of guilt, no stress hormones, no negativity, and your body assimilates the food differently, healthfully. Now, I'm not suggesting we eat cake every day because we love ourselves so damn much, but you see, that would never happen anyway because of the first example. When we love ourselves, it changes our behavior to make better choices, and when we choose better, we live better. Eating cake every day would be inconsistent with your self-loving identity, and you wouldn't have the urge to do something that's harmful to yourself.

But that's not all. Daily loving and acceptance of yourself also *infuses you with health.* Your cells become happy, and proteins and hormones zoom around your body, helping you be healthy, bolstering your immune system, reducing inflammation, and rebuilding for a strong future. When your self-esteem is boosted and your self-love soars—both results from your Coffee Self-Talk—

weight can start to come off without even changing your eating or fitness habits, through metabolic changes alone! It's weird, but the brain has a way of making things real, especially when it comes to your body, metabolism, gene expression, immunity, and health in general.

Here's another example: You don't wait to find someone to love you before loving *yourself first*. When you love yourself first, just watch as someone wonderful comes into your life, as if by magic. Loving people are attracted to loving people. When you send out the right energy, other people will notice and find it irresistible.

Another example: You don't wait for a crisis to happen to trigger you to improve your life or remake it. Instead, you'll become grateful for every breath you take now, loving and appreciating yourself, and your life, as you are today. If you're living a decent life, with no major complaints, then don't wait for something bad to happen to take action. Dig your well before you're thirsty! Coffee Self-Talk is the way to get on it now!

There are no excuses for not beginning today. Here's a rule to live by:

Loving yourself is a prerequisite to getting everything you want in life.

If you want to thrive, if you want to feel amazing and powerful and full of energy, and if you want to glide through your life with more ease, then start loving yourself. Today. Using Coffee Self-Talk.

Something amazing happens once we start to love ourselves. Everything brightens, becomes more vibrant, and you feel agile, stronger. It's as though an invisible weight is lifted off your shoulders when you give yourself permission to take what is your birthright: *the freedom to pursue your own destiny.* Happiness. You feel better instantly, no matter what is going on in life. An injury? A breakup? A pandemic? A layoff? A hurtful deceit? That's OK, because loving yourself keeps you feeling whole. Loving yourself keeps you feeling worthy. When you feel whole and worthy, you're absolutely *unlimited*.

Unstoppable. You're worthy and magnificent, deserving the best that life has to offer.

If we start with loving ourselves, we create an energy, a wonderful, uplifting vibe. It surrounds you and extends beyond you. It becomes the nutrient-rich soil that grows the self-talk seeds you sow. Self-love makes your self-talk more powerful. It attracts the right people, the right opportunities, and the right circumstances into your life.

Initially, loving yourself might seem hard to do. But that's where Coffee Self-Talk comes into play and guides you. While doing your daily self-talk, you're pumping yourself up, changing the wiring in your brain, and in turn, starting to love yourself. It might not feel like that the first time you sit down to read your Coffee Self-Talk, but after a few times, it will start to take root. You planted seeds, you watered and nourished them through repetition, and the sprouts begin to take root. Soon, you'll start noticing that your life just seems to get better and better, and your possibilities and opportunities grow. Perhaps slowly at first, but then bigger and bigger. Small successes beget confidence, and confidence begets big successes, in an upward spiral that grows exponentially.

Benefit #3: Coffee Self-Talk for Happiness

As you now know, self-talk greatly boosts your self-esteem, well-being, and zest for life. And that these, in turn, heal and improve your body and your mind. It bears repeating, so you never forget—positive self-talk makes people tremendously happier.

Happiness exists in the moment. That's important to remember because it means you can tap into it any time you choose. But when you do this all the time, you create a continuous flow of happy moments, like a happiness IV (intravenous) drip... which creates a long-term *pattern of happiness*. And this creates a stellar life in general. Research shows that happier people are more productive, more helpful, more active, and more likable. They're also less stressed. So be one of those happy guys who always somehow seems to be more resilient, healthier, more creative, and make more money. You know, the kind of guy who always seems to be lucky.

Newsflash: *It ain't luck!*

So let's get started getting happier, because your happiness is all in your own mind. It's totally up to you. No matter what's going on around you, no matter what your circumstances, no matter what crap happened to you as a kid, or yesterday at work, or 10 minutes ago. The way you react and move forward is 100% UP TO YOU.

Benefit #4: Coffee Self-Talk for Resilience

You'll find that your self-talk is a healthy and "protective" habit because your emotions are easier to keep in check and not easily perturbed by external events or your own random thoughts. Your self-esteem becomes too strong for that. External conditions and opinions will have less weight as your internal value (your self-esteem) increases. When this happens, bullets bounce off you (well, the metaphorical kind), giving you the strength and resilience to get up again and keep on going. Like the Japanese proverb says, *fall down seven times, get up eight*. That's resilience. It comes from inside.

This flexibility, this endurance you'll have... they are some of the most important benefits of Coffee Self-Talk. It's like you're wearing armor. And you know you're wearing it, such that you gain the courage and confidence to strive, reach higher, and take risks. Like having the confidence to ask that special someone out on a date, to ask for that raise you deserve, to post that video on YouTube, launch that business, or show off your talent on open-mic night. Or hey, even writing that novel! Either way, you're no longer afraid of rejection, and you actually look forward to attempting new challenges and learning from them.

This applies to me in spades. As an author, loving myself from my self-talk allows me to keep my spirits aloft despite... *eek!*... book reviews! Do you know how easy it can be to let one negative review from a total stranger ruin your whole day? Even when it's just a lone, weird opinion in a sea of good reviews, it still sucks and can trigger a slippery slope into despair. But when your self-esteem is high and you love yourself, you don't mind people's opinions. You're protected from them, and you're even equipped to consider the criticism objectively, unemotionally, in case there's anything there that might help you improve.

Benefit #5: Coffee Self-Talk for Love, Money, and Health

Coffee Self-Talk genuinely improves your life in so many ways, but the big three buckets are:

- Love
- Health
- Money

I discuss these more in coming chapters, but suffice it to say, Coffee Self-Talk can help you find a life-long love or relationship—you know, the kind in movies—because it helps you to be your authentic self, and *that* helps you attract your soulmate, someone who resonates with the *real* you.

Self-talk is used by many to improve health, whether healing from a disease or injury, getting into great shape, or simply improving your overall well-being (see Chapters 14–16).

And self-talk can also benefit your bank account, increasing your wealth and abundance as your confidence and creativity soar (see Chapter 17). You see more opportunities and doors opening. It also makes you spend more wisely, focusing on what really makes you happy.

Benefit #6: Coffee Self-Talk to Manifest Your Dreams Faster

The reason I'm militant about making my self-talk a daily habit is because, when I decided to become a *Happy Sexy Millionaire*, I aimed to manifest it ASAP. And nothing makes things happen faster than consistent, daily progress toward a goal.

Self-talk is a vital component to manifesting my Happy Sexy Millionaire destiny. It's one of my tools for keeping my attitude and self-esteem boosted. It keeps me chugging forward like a freight train. Every. Single. Day. As I've learned along my Happy Sexy Millionaire journey, and as I'll share a bit later, a critical component to the Law of Attraction (and manifesting your dreams) is to maintain elevated emotions throughout your day, and nothing I've found makes this easier than Coffee Self-Talk.

Merely thinking about the dreamy awesome life you want, and the goals to get there, isn't the fastest way to make it all happen. It turns out that just coming up with a list of wants and desires puts you in the slowpoke lane to abundance. It's not a dead end, but it's not a rocket sled ride either.

The magic happens when you combine those ideas, goals, and life ambitions with *elevated emotions*—where you feel unlimited, excited, and full of love. It's this union between the *thinking* and *feeling* parts of your brain that creates coherence in your thoughts and actions, removes all the bullshit barriers (like self-doubt), and puts you in the seat of a Formula One car, racing toward your future legendary life.

You see, when your heart is filled with these uplifted emotions, there is no room for fear. Just imagine how your life would feel if you felt *no fear*. As Frank Herbert said, *fear is the mind-killer*. I used to bathe in fear. Now, it's virtually gone. The difference in my life between then and now is absolutely astonishing, and I'm never going back.

Benefit #7: Coffee Self-Talk Creates a New Legendary You

Picture this: You... building toward your dreams, feeling bold, confident, and happy. How awesome would that be? How different would your life be if you felt like you were sailing through it smiling, instead of slogging and trudging? How much more would you accomplish every day, week, or month if you had more energy, verve, and confidence? Think about all of those things, because it's about to happen with your new Coffee Self-Talk program.

The positive affirmations and thoughts you say and think are commands to your subconscious. They're a blueprint for your brain. As you fill your head with these thoughts, they become your habits, you make new choices, and create an incredible new, magical version of you—of your design!

Do you ever wish you were more of one thing or another? Do you wonder what it would be like if you were braver, or funnier, or more creative? Do you wish you were a better writer? Do you want to lose weight? Be stronger? Do you want to be more relaxed and not so anxious? Well, you can change your personality and attitude with regular self-talk specifically designed to make you become the person you dream of becoming.

It really works. I'm living proof, as are the millions of people who do it. Coffee Self-Talk has made me happier. It's made me a better writer. It's motivated me to get to the gym on days I didn't think I wanted to go. It's made me a better parent. It's made me a more romantic spouse. The list goes on, and you can experience the same results.

Benefit #8: Coffee Self-Talk for Confidence

I mentioned confidence above, but I want to be more specific, because this is a big one. Self-talk has increased my own confidence to such a healthy degree, that I now easily talk with strangers, striking up conversations more comfortably than ever before. Even in *Italy,* where I don't yet speak the language very well—I approach people with no fear about screwing up or being misunderstood. This not only helps me learn more (Italian, in my case), but it also opens up many new opportunities. Sometimes I learn things or meet people that solve an immediate problem in my own life, or I tap into a whole new network of people from a single conversation with one stranger. Or I discover a way I can help them with something, or maybe I just make a new friend. It's always a win.

Coffee Self-Talk also enables loving myself through any stress and anxiety, creating a safe place to be, instantly. When I used to write a blog post or publish a book, rather than feeling joy from my accomplishment, anxiety laced my experience. Because, once my written content was out there, I felt vulnerable. I wondered how it would be received. I kept checking social media with squinted eyes... did people like it?

To hell with that! Now, I courageously push my art out into the world with joy and excitement. I've conditioned my mind to know I'm a prolific writer with value to offer. And that it comes from an unlimited wellspring of creativity. I can keep creating, non-stop, because there's no lack of ideas. I just keep telling myself that—and it works!

I no longer worry about other people's reactions. Some people will like it and some people won't. The people who like it are my audience; those who don't aren't. For my part, I'm having so much damn fun writing and sharing, that I'm excited and eager to keep doing it.

Once you've reprogrammed yourself to be confident, you no longer consciously think about it. It becomes your "new normal," your new way of being. This is when true mastery and power are at your fingertips. Your default mindset becomes one of flexibility and confidence. Like a palm tree in a tropical storm, it stays rooted, effortlessly bending in the wind—dancing—until the howling wind passes. These things allow you to handle any situation and resist fear. It's epic. It's game-changing.

Benefit #9: Coffee Self-Talk Future-Proofing

Coffee Self-Talk also "future-proofs" you. When you increase your confidence, and you experience the feelings that come with it, you minimize the effects of shocks and stresses of future events. As I mentioned before, confidence begets success, and success begets confidence, in a virtuous cycle. Coffee Self-Talk jump-starts that cycle. It starts building your bulletproof armor immediately. But stick with it for a while, and you become so badass, you'll be bomb-proof.

All this by making simple statements to yourself. Words. Your words.

In this book, you'll learn how to make your own Coffee Self-Talk, so you can tap into all of these incredible benefits. I'll give you ideas for what to say in your self-talk, including unique enhancements I personally use to make my daily ritual even more effective than just saying the words. I promise, if you spend the time to sit down and enjoy a cup of coffee, reading through your self-talk, and stick with it, you will have an amazing life.

Very little is needed to make a happy life. It is all within yourself, in your way of thinking.

— MARCUS AURELIUS

Chapter 4

THE SCIENCE BEHIND THE MAGIC OF SELF-TALK

The mind and body are one. We all have far more control over our health and well-being than we realize.

— Ellen Langer, Harvard Psychologist, "The Mother of Mindfulness"

Self-talk actually changes your brain's physical structure. Human brains are *neuroplastic*, which simply means they can change in drastic ways, no matter how old you are. It's how we learn new skills, like playing the piano, or archery, or learning a new language, or in my case, writing fiction.

But it also means our thought patterns can change, too, such as how we look at the world or respond to things that happen. Neuroscientists have confirmed that our brains remain super flexible, and you can build new neural pathways. When you learn new things, your brain's cells (called neurons) take action! You're the director, they're the actors. You're the general. They're the soldiers under your command; they do whatever you tell them to do.

This is important because it's how Coffee Self-Talk is going to help you get unstuck, and on the right trajectory to creating your legendary life. Because you—*you!*—determine what takes root (or doesn't) inside your head, based on what you're thinking and feeling in every moment. Coffee Self-Talk gives you that control.

Fire It Up to Wire It Up: The Baked-In Mindset

When you do something or feel something repeatedly, it becomes baked into your mindset. More specifically, your brain cells "fire and wire" with the thoughts you have. This means they activate by firing with a certain thought pattern, and every time they fire together, because of repeating this pattern, the neurons start to connect, or "wire together."

The more this happens—or the more emotion that accompanies the wiring—the stronger the connection. Do this enough times, and the pattern becomes deeply ingrained, as though the wires were thicker and stronger. This essentially changes the structure of your brain. It also makes you *who you are*—your personality.

If you pay attention to this process, you have control over it. You can do it any time you choose. New thought patterns, beliefs, behaviors, habits—done repeatedly, will fire and wire to create a new life, whenever you want. You have the control, and it all comes from your thoughts, behaviors, and feelings. New thinking? New You!

The more your neurons fire together in a pattern, the stronger they wire together. The stronger the wires, the more pronounced they are. And the harder they are to dismantle, meaning they become resilient and permanent. That's good when wiring good things. And, well, bad when wiring bad things, such as shitty habits or negative beliefs about yourself, or the world, that might not even be true. But once you recognize these, you CAN change them.

Why This Superpower Is of Vital Importance

The ability to rewire your brain is important because it's how you become a new you! It's how you create your legendary life and experience happiness and joy *as your default mode*. In other words, this becomes your new norm. It means you don't wait for something to happen outside yourself to feel good, because you have the recipe and ingredients for change inside you at all times. This is our superpower, and anyone can do it!

Coffee Self-Talk helped me reprogram my brain for high-performance and success, and it will do the same for you. Instead of waking up tired, groggy, or without focus, I now leap out of bed with a force that projects me excitedly into a brand-new day. When I look back to the mornings of my past, they're so different than my experience now. Even during the time of the coronavirus pandemic, my days were filled with joy and purpose. Those conditions, though they uprooted my life temporarily, did nothing to shake my bliss that came from a deep reserve inside me.

I can't say it enough: With the right mindset, words, and thoughts, you, too, will tap into a wellspring of joy, no matter what is going on around you.

"Pruning Shears"—A Tool Your Brain Uses to Help You

The cool thing is that, as you fire and wire your new kick-ass thought patterns, over time, the old wiring withers away because you're using it less. Connections in your brain literally atrophy from disuse, just like muscles. As the old saying goes, "use it or lose it."

In other words, the more good things you say and think, the more your brain changes to support those things, while getting rid of the old, unused connections. When this happens in the brain, neuroscientists call it "pruning," which is a wonderful metaphor... just imagine all the old, bad garbage being pruned away, like dead or weak branches on a tree, providing more nutrients and energy to all the healthy branches. *Snip. Snip. Snip.*

This is great when reprogramming your subconscious for your legendary life, because once your new wiring is strong from repetition, it'll be very hard (or impossible) for the old negative patterns to creep back in. With enough time, provided you keep up your positive self-talk, there's no fear of backsliding to your old self. That badass you've become has gone through a one-way metamorphosis, so there's no turning back into a limp, squishy caterpillar. Even if old triggers pop up out of nowhere, they'll have no power over you anymore. The old limiting crap—beliefs, ideas, thoughts, etc.—eventually go silent and don't bother you. Isn't that a relief?

As this happens, your brain starts dismantling that old shitty wiring, in order to reuse those building blocks for the awesome, new, active circuits you're creating. The new you! So, as you're learning new things, you're changing the person you are because your brain is constantly dismantling the old and creating the new, in real time. You get what you repeat. It's not "you are what you eat." It's "you are what you *think!*"

Just Imagine… Having a Dramatically Different Brain Than the One You've Got Now

Neuroscience shows that your brain can physically and chemically change with each and every new thought you think, emotion you feel, and experience you have. Huge transformations can occur in just a few weeks, no matter your age or circumstances!

Here's an example. As I think great thoughts and feel elevated emotions (love, awe, gratitude, etc.), I'm firing and wiring the good stuff. This can be as simple as thinking about my husband and daughter, feeling love for them. Or thinking about the food I get to eat and feeling gratitude. Or staring in wonder at the mountains or the ocean and feeling awe. Or chilling with my dog and feeling peace.

Or standing in my own power, knowing I am capable and awesome. Or thinking with excited anticipation about the future I'm designing and feeling unlimited.

All of these moments of feeling elevated emotions are groovin' and wiring my brain for success, prosperity, love, and everything good. Call it "upwiring" your brain, because it's an upgrade! Moreover, as I'm doing this, I'm *no longer* running my old fear-based circuitry (created in my childhood), and so it starts to wither away over time. How cool!

But It's Not Just About Your Brain

Until now, I've been emphasizing how self-talk rewires your brain. But it goes beyond this, because your brain controls so much of what's happening in your body. In fact, your brain can literally *change* your body. This means self-talk can change your body, too!

Did you know there is research showing that what you think can change your physical body without actually doing anything physical? That's how powerful our minds are. Researchers have done studies where people *imagine* themselves flexing a muscle, and they achieve *actual physical strength gains*—without having lifted a finger! Like—um, wtf? Mind blown! Who needs a gym when you can just tap into the matrix of your mind and get buff? Hehe.

But seriously, the subjects in this study were activating pathways in their brains related to movement, so their brains thought they were physically moving when they weren't. When hooked up to MRIs to image what was happening inside the brain, the imaging depicted the same activity whether the muscles lifted real weight or not. This is phenomenal!

Here's an incredible example of how powerful our minds really are. In Dr. Joe Dispenza's book, *You Are the Placebo*, he shares an example of how the mind can change the body's reaction to an allergic substance. In Japan, there was a study of 13 boys who were hypersensitive to a plant with effects similar to poison ivy. The researchers touched the students on one arm with leaves from a tree *that was harmless*, but the researchers told the boys that these leaves were actually poisonous leaves. As a result, all 13 arms touched with the harmless leaves showed a skin reaction even though the leaves were not poisonous. *But the boys believed they were!*

Then, the researchers touched the boys on the opposite arm *with poisonous leaves,* but this time, they told the boys these leaves were harmless. This time, only two of the thirteen boys touched with the poisonous leaves had an allergic reaction. Eleven of the thirteen boys had no reaction because they thought the leaves were harmless.

Skeptical? It gets even better. Consider the case of Timmy, a boy who has no problem drinking orange juice. But Timmy shares the brain of a young boy with multiple personality disorder. When any of the boy's eleven other personalities drink orange juice, the boy breaks out in hives. Even weirder, when Timmy returns, the itching ceases immediately, and the water-filled blisters gradually disappear.

Whoa.

It sounds nuts, but is it really? Isn't the brain just a master regulator of chemical signals—neurotransmitters and hormones? When Timmy's around, some chemical switch gets flipped, and his body simply follows those new directions.

Your brain does the same thing. That's the kind of power we all yield with our very own minds. It's time to start flipping some switches.

Multiply to Amplify

Whether the thoughts you think are good or bad, when you repeat them, they gain momentum and strength. Hence, "multiply to amplify." Because repetition is equally effective at amplifying both good and bad thoughts, be sure to choose GOOD!

Each time we repeat the good words, their emotional value becomes greater, creating more powerful feelings behind them. When this happens, you'd better watch out—*BAM!*—because your brain and body launch into action to create your luminous new reality.

Your thoughts work like compound interest for manifesting your new life. The effects multiply as you repeat them. So be smart and choose wisely every thought circulating around your head (and every feeling circulating around your body), because each one matters. (In fact, your self-talk thoughts literally *become matter*.)

If you're someone who complains and whines, it's not helping you. At all. If you wake up feeling like you're under a mountain of to-do's, debt, or seemingly suffocating circumstances, it's time to not only change your perspective (I'll provide some tricks for this later), but to just shush those thoughts by not even giving them a chance to make an appearance. Stop living under a cloak of darkness. If you do, you're wasting your life!

Those thoughts are negative affirmations, and every time you think or say one of them, those bad pathways in your brain get stronger. They're called affirmations because that's what they do—they affirm something as though it's truth! So we're going to crowd out the negative crap-talk with our empowering positive-talk and *alternative perspective techniques* (APT)—see Chapter 10. You'll see that real changes occur as a result.

Perpetual optimism is a force multiplier.

— COLIN POWELL

Our beliefs can heal us—mentally and physically. But they can also harm us. If you're the person who says, "I always get the flu when it comes around." Guess what? You're creating the environment to make that statement true as often as possible. (This is currently a hot topic in science. In fact, there is an entire field called psychoneuroimmunology, which studies the chemical pathways our brains use to modify our immune systems, making us more or less resistant to disease. This isn't hocus pocus and voodoo... it's neurotransmitters, hormones, and epigenetics.)

Our words are extremely powerful. Our neuroplastic brains make it all possible because our brains have the ability to change. Your mind —and therefore, your personality, and your reality—are not static. But what's really amazing is how quickly change can happen. Your brain can change in a second, with a single thought, and that means you can instantly change the direction of your life. Coffee Self-Talk, done on a regular basis, will create a healthy mindset that is automatic, effortless, and completely natural. Your great attitude will become your habitual way—like a badass skill!

I'm sure you've heard the old sayings, "people don't change" or "you can't teach an old dog new tricks." Well, these are generally true, in the sense that most people *don't know* they can change, and so they don't even make the attempt. But strictly speaking, these statements are completely false. People can and DO change. You CAN learn new tricks, at any age. Dr. Helmstetter himself picked up a bow and arrow for the first time in his seventies. He's now an accomplished archer with Olympic-level skill. Now *that's* neuroplasticity!

So, under the right conditions, anybody can change. And best of all, you can start *immediately.*

The mind is everything. What you think, you become.

— THE BUDDHA

Chapter 5

YOUR COFFEE SELF-TALK

Right now, you stand in your very own rich power, no matter where you are, no matter what the circumstances in your life. Feel the pages of your life turning now. It's your time. You have the potential and authority to change your beliefs about yourself, today. You have the right to make a better choice in every moment. It's all about the thoughts you think about yourself and the world. Reprogram your brain for the best, and you'll reap the rewards. Now is your time.

In this chapter, I cover the basics for writing your own Coffee Self-Talk from scratch. If you prefer not to write your own, or if you'd like to use pre-written examples to get started right away, many scripts are provided for you in Part II of this book.

The Coffee Self-Talk Rules

Rule #1: Write in First Person

Always write, speak, and think your self-talk in the first person. Example:

I feel generous with my success,
and I eagerly share with others.

First person is necessary for making "you" both the giver and receiver of the programs that will rewire your brain. It's the easiest way to get straight into your own head, feeling it faster. You're telling your story in your words, in your voice. "I" is the *self* in self-talk.

Rule #2: Write in the Present Tense

The second trick to creating powerful self-talk is to write it in the present tense. This creates a sense that it has already happened, or it's happening now. Not tomorrow, not next month, not next year. Do this even if the thing you want hasn't happened yet. Remember, you're doing this to reprogram your brain. You want your brain to start acting as though the thing you want has already become reality. You don't want to give your brain any excuses to put things off until "later."

So, write and speak your self-talk as though there's no time between saying it and when it happens. No space between you and your accomplishments and feeling good.

The things you write in your Coffee Self-Talk will range from accomplishments you see yourself making, to ways to make it happen, to how it all makes you feel. It's your epic new truth, and you're attracting your desires by positively affirming it all.

Get Your Magic Wand Ready

A great way to brainstorm about writing your own Coffee Self-Talk script is to start by thinking about your life now versus the life you want. If you could wave a magic wand and make changes to yourself or your life, what would you do?

Do you want a better job? Would you like to find love? Do you wish you had more confidence? Do you want to heal from a disease or injury? Do you want to lose weight or find the motivation to work out? Do you want to like exercise? Do you want to start a good habit like meditation? Do you want to break a bad habit like sugar or alcohol? Do you wish you were funnier? Wealthier? Happier? More creative?

Think about what you want, who you want to become, how you want to live, and how you want to feel.

Ask yourself the following questions:

- What are all the things that expand my energy?
- How can I have more of those things in my life?
- What three things or people bring me pure joy?
- What is my favorite past time?
- Where is my favorite place to vacation?
- What do I want more of?
- What do I want less of?
- What do I want that I don't have now?
- How will it make me feel to have the things I want?

Write down anything and everything that pops into your mind. Then, take those dreams and write them in phrases and affirmative statements using words like "I love _____," and "I am _____," and "I feel _____," etc. (See the scripts below for examples.)

The Coffee Self-Talk Daily Process

Once you've written your self-talk (or you've selected one of the provided scripts), you'll read it to yourself (preferably out loud) every morning, while having your cup of coffee.

Again, it might feel weird or strange talking to yourself, and about yourself, but don't worry. I promise it will quickly become super easy and fun. You'll soon become accustomed to the sound of talking to yourself, about yourself. In fact, it'll become so normal, you'll soon *never* tolerate a bad thought or word about yourself. You'll be struck by just how wrong it feels, like sandpaper rubbing on satin.

The more you speak your self-talk out loud, the easier it is to do. It becomes fun and natural, and you'll look forward to it. You'll crave it like you crave your coffee. As it feeds your brain and mind with super-charged mental nutrients, you might even start to feel tingly, in awe, and amped up to the sky. It feels so good. If you have any moments of doubt or weird feelings, simply observe the thought, and say, "Thanks for stopping by, thought." And then keep going, because that's how you win!

Get Started Now—Simple Starting Script

Here are two examples for a general, non-specific Coffee Self-Talk script. In this first example, I'm going to start with gentle and effective words. You can type this into your own Notes app or anything else, like Evernote, or a written journal.

Later, we'll elevate the following script to more intense and impactful words, but this lighter example will give you some ideas to get started if you're totally new to self-love and boosting your self-esteem.

Get your cup of coffee and sit down to read through it. Pause after each one for a couple of seconds, to let it sink in.

(Email me at Kristen@KristenHelmstetter.com to get a free, printable PDF of the Coffee Self-Talk scripts in this book.)

I am a good person.

I like today.

I feel uplifted right now, because I'm taking care of me.

I love life.

I love my life because it has direction and meaning.

I will have a good day today because I'm ready.

My income is increasing, and only good lies before me.

I bless everything in my life right now. My coffee, my chair, my home, my life.

I like feeling good.

I approve of myself because I'm truly great.

I love the power I have in my life to feel good with simple words.

I achieve because I persevere.

I choose to feel good about myself because I'm worthy.

I stand in my own power.

All is wonderful today.

I always have a choice.

I'm healthy and wealthy.

I have time for everything I want to do today.

I feel terrific.

I have an incredible attitude.

Today is a great day.

I love me just the way I am, today.

I'm tapping into good feelings right now because that's the key to success.

This is fun, and I'm ready for my day.

Life is full of opportunities because I am open to them.

I am healthy and full of vitality.

I feel really good right now because I love my life.

Are You Feeling Silly About This?

I'll be honest, the first time I did this, I felt like such a nerd... but only for about a minute. Then, I thought about all of the ridiculously successful people out there tooting a similar horn, marching in the same band. Using self-talk is not new, and there are legions of people using it to kick major ass, make tons of money, heal from diseases, achieve super fitness, and live incredible lives.

I wanted a piece of that, and realizing this is one of the ways you can transform and take life to new heights, I was all-in. I threw off my metaphorical taped nerd-glasses and donned my superhero cape. Game on!

The interesting thing was seeing how my Coffee Self-Talk scripts evolved over time. In the beginning, my scripts were much like the script you just read above. Now though, I pump myself up so high, I damn near feel I'm levitating when I read it! I *really* get into it.

Now It's Your Turn

The first time you sit to read your Coffee Self-Talk script, it might only take one minute to complete. If this happens, and you still have coffee in your cup, simply read it again. And again. And again. Rinse and repeat. Keep going, until you're done with your coffee. Then, go about the rest of your day feeling uplifted, more confident, and with a positive focus.

As you grow in your Coffee Self-Talk, you'll likely find your script getting longer. It's so damn fun and inspiring. It's as addictive as the caffeine you're drinking while doing it. At first, many people start out with basics and simple generalizations. Over time, you'll flesh out your script (or scripts) by adding specific details that are relevant to you, your situation, and your goals.

New ideas and descriptions will start to flourish in your mind. The more you think about the amazing life you're living, the more ideas come to you. You'll find yourself during random moments of the day having an idea, or a flash of insight, and wanting to jot it down in your notes to add to your script later. Be sure and do this whenever the inspiration strikes!

The details you add to your scripts are important. They create a more vivid picture in your head, making it crystal clear. For example, you might add a few lines tailored to healthy eating habits. You might add a line about the abundance you feel in your life, and how it has changed your outlook, or the decisions you make. You might add an empowering lyric from your favorite song that keeps you laser-focused on the new you. Or you could write a line about doing something physical daily, like a set of push-ups, to keep that picture front and center in your mind.

You'll eventually get to the point where you spend five, 10, or maybe 15 minutes per day reviewing your Coffee Self-Talk script. It evolves, as it should. My script is so long now, that it takes a full 20 minutes to go through, depending on how cinematic I feel like getting (more on theatrics later). But I don't care about the length of time. I freakin' love every minute of it. It makes me high.

Then there are some days when I only get partway through as I finish my coffee, and I pick it up later. Other times, I sit there with the whole thing, soaking it all in, luxuriating in *two* cups of coffee. The point is, I'm doing it. Every. Damn. Day.

Later in this book, you'll discover more ways to enhance your Coffee Self-Talk to catapult it to crazy-cool levels. For now, the first simple step is to write 15 easy and powerful self-talk statements.

Amping It Up! A More Advanced Script to Level-Up Your Coffee Self-Talk

The basic script above is a great way to get started. Take it and use every word, or make any changes to it that resonate with you. I tend to use the words "awesome" and "amazing" a lot for my own Coffee

Self-Talk, and my father-in-law uses "incredible" a lot. Choose something that works for you. You can also make your script longer or shorter... whatever length you want. Heck, it can even be just one statement that you repeat over and over. A concentrated mantra, small yet mighty... like *Espresso Self-Talk!*

Once you get started, it's fun, and you'll be so excited about the possibilities, that you'll start thinking of new ways to speak powerfully and positively about yourself. You'll start thinking and speaking in this new form of language naturally. Unleash your most energizing words, thoughts, and dreams. Don't be shy—it's your time to shine!

Here's the more amped-up version, dense with power words:

I am an amazing person because I am kind and generous.

I love today because I'm in charge of my day. I make it what I want! I am powerful.

I feel uplifted right now, in this very moment, because I'm taking care of me. I deserve this time to prepare for my day and make it the best day ever.

I love life. I love my life. I love me! Life is full of opportunities everywhere I turn. I'm going for it!

I'm having an awesome day today! I smile brightly, and I'm excited about everything happening today, hour by hour.

I let go of all fear, right now. I'm taking responsibility for my success, now, and for the rest of my life.

I bless everything in my life right now. My coffee, my chair, my bed, my family, my friends, my whole life.

I LOVE feeling so awesome! Yesssssssss!!!

Yesterday is the past, and I'm not attached to it. I learn from it and move on.

I'm ready to love me today—here and now. This creates a great moment for me and sets up my future for more success.

Doors of opportunity are opening all around me. I'm jazzed about them.

I love the power I have in my life to feel so super, simply with the words I speak. I am amazing.

I can achieve because I'm capable, creative, and worthy. I choose me, and I honor who I am.

My life gets more amazing every day. Life supports me in every way.

I approve of myself. I let go of limited thinking and beliefs.

All is wonderful today. I am in awe of my powerful life, my learning, and my growth.

I have an abundance of time for everything I want to do today.

I feel terrific because I am whole, healthy, and full of vitality.

Today is an incredible day, and I'm tapping into powerful, amped-up feelings right now. Feeling it!

This is fun, and I love being so playful. I am strong and bold.

There is love and light all around me. I am compassionate, kind, and respectful toward myself and others.

There is nothing I can't do. I have a happy heart and a creative mind. My thoughts are positive, and my feelings are uplifted. This creates my most amazing life.

I'm brilliant, and I love to learn.

There is no one else in the world like me.

I am one sexy motherfucker!

I'm living a completely new life of my own creative design.

I am full of optimism and passionate about my destiny.

Pro-Tip #1: Use the Word "Because" for More Success

Example: *"I have no problem making it to the gym every scheduled day* **because** *I know how great exercise makes me feel."*

Using the word "because" is a smart way to enhance your self-talk, and this is backed up by scientific studies demonstrating its power. When you use (or hear) the word "because," you're more likely to comply with what's being said or asked of you. The words that come after "because" provide the reason to do it. It justifies motivation for the action because it indicates a strong cause-and-effect relationship.

As a result, your brain pays attention when you use the word "because," and you give more importance to the self-talk. When you associate results and meaning with your self-talk, you're more convinced it'll help you achieve your self-talk goals. So, set yourself up for success, and sprinkle the word "because" throughout your script, *because* it will really help.

Pro-Tip #2: Spark Joy with Details

Get creative and play with the words you're using. They can, and should, change over time because your Coffee Self-Talk evolves. When I write my self-talk, I first write whatever comes to mind. Then, I edit, tweaking each statement until it sparks joy with me. Like Marie Kondo, author of *The Life-Changing Art of Tidying Up,* says about possessions: Does the object (dresser, shirt, vase, etc.) spark joy? If not, get rid of it. Or in the case of writing self-talk, edit it down until everything that remains sparks joy inside you.

For example, I wanted a phrase about aging... *backwards.* I played with phrases like "anti-aging," "reverse aging," etc., but I soon realized I didn't want to use the word "aging" in any way. It's not uplifting for me, even with "anti-" before it. It sounds too stodgy and therapeutic. So I continued writing it different ways, to see how different sentences resonated with me. The evolution went like this... "I am aging backwards." "I am anti-aging." "My anti-aging genes are expressing themselves right now." "I look and feel young." Hmm... this is getting close.

"I am young and beautiful." That's it! Joy was sparked. *Ding-ding.* I found a phrase I loved, and that sparked that special feeling in me. It felt *right.* For you, it might be "I am young and full of vigor," or "I am young in body, wise in mind," etc. Play with the words until they click for you.

But then I went deeper with it. I started writing more specifics. The more details I gave my brain, the easier it would be for it to follow my directions. Our brains love words that evoke mental images, and if we can present pictures for the mind, then it's easier for our brain and body to make it happen. So, I also wrote "My body makes ample collagen, and my skin is perfect, smooth, and glowing."

I ended up liking and keeping both sentences. I wrote:

I am young and beautiful. My body makes ample collagen, and my skin is perfect, smooth, and glowing.

As a male, you might try something like:

I am young and full of vigor. My body recovers quickly, my joints glide with ease, and I have the stamina of an 18-year-old.

So, you can see how the idea for anti-aging was something I wanted to have in my Coffee Self-Talk, and by rewriting it until I resonated deeply with it, I created a more powerful affirmation. Our brains like clarity, so as your Coffee Self-Talk evolves, don't be shy about using powerful words and descriptive details to create distinctive pictures of exactly what you want.

Here's another example. I started with:

My life is full of abundance.

That's good, simple, and positive. But kind of vague, so I went deeper. I started picturing precisely what "abundance" meant for me. From that single sentence, my abundance script ended up as:

> *My life has an abundance of time to do everything I want. I have abundant, radiant health. I'm full of vitality and energy, and I bounce out of bed every morning. I have an abundance of wealth, and opportunities are all around me for making metric shit-tons of money.*

As you can see, I increased the idea of simple abundance and gave it more rich detail, while still keeping my Coffee Self-Talk simple and to the point. There's no need to get super intricate, unless it resonates with you to be that way! I like to start with easy and simple statements, and then I increase the descriptive words, while still keeping the theme sharp and to-the-point.

The funny thing is, once you start writing or thinking of your self-talk statements, it may seem overwhelming because there are so many great things to say, improve, or change. You may find the floodgates open, as you imagine all kinds of inspiring, awesome things to say, think, and feel. At one time, my daily Coffee Self-Talk script took me over 30 minutes to go through because I was covering so much territory! (When I first started, my daily general script took only five minutes, and I gradually added to it. It currently takes me about 20 minutes, or 5–10 if I'm in a hurry. Scripts covering specific topics, like writing, only take about five minutes.)

The main point is for you to imagine whatever awesome life you want, and then write your Coffee Self-Talk to reflect those thoughts, in the present tense, like they're already happening. If your floodgates do open, don't worry, just capture as much as you can in writing (or dictation), and you can always pare it down later. When your muse is on a rampage, get the hell out of its way!

Over time, keep adding to your script whenever you're inspired. If there's one particular statement you feel closest too, then just put that statement on repeat, and say it over and over, like a commanding mantra. It'll become trance-like and pop into your head at random times throughout the day, jolting you like a little electric current of happiness and confidence.

Sometimes when I'm listening to music, I'll hear a lyric that would make a great line in my Coffee Self-Talk, so I add it!

Whatever your source of inspiration, be creative, and have fun finding all the ways to say empowering and inspiring things to yourself.

> *The greatest discovery of any generation is that a human being can alter his life by altering his attitude.*
>
> — WILLIAM JAMES

Chapter 6

HOW TO DO YOUR COFFEE SELF-TALK

From the previous chapter, you know how to write your Coffee Self-Talk script. That's the first part of the process. Now it's time to learn how to actually do the self-talk.

The KEY to Successful Coffee Self-Talk: Aligning Feelings with Thoughts

The analytical brain tends to undervalue the role of feelings. But suppressed feelings don't go away, they go underground, operating on our subconscious mind in powerful, sometimes sneaky ways. Our emotions emerge from anatomical structures in our brain that have been fine-tuned by natural selection over a hundred thousand years to keep us alive. Ignore them at your peril... they're *very* important. Our emotions operate like a shadow operating system inside our skulls. They're like a black-box computer, sifting through petabytes of data from our senses and memories, calculating odds, and generating responses, which manifest as instincts and intuitions. This is where your "gut feel" comes from.

The most powerful people in history, from Napoleon to Steve Jobs, learned how to listen to this alternate computational system, and then filter the results of their intuition through analytical rigor. A blending of right and left-brain approaches to problem solving.

Creative brilliance also comes from your emotions. It's called *ideation* —or coming up with ideas, good or bad. Good strategies come from blending creativity with cold-blooded vetting, which rejects the bad ideas, and highlights the good. Brilliant thinkers learn to cultivate both of these systems, and use them in tandem.

One of the most important ways to make your self-talk successful is to elevate the feelings that accompany the words you say. This is mission-critical, so let's dive into the concept.

The words you say (or think) when doing your self-talk *have power in proportion to the level of elevated emotion you feel* when you're saying or thinking them.

Let me restate this another way...

The words you say are as important as how you feel, and how you feel is as important as the words you say. If words are peanut butter, then feelings are jelly. If words are peas, then feelings are carrots. If words are Humphrey Bogart, then feelings are Lauren Bacall. It takes two to tango. It's a marriage. We want them both!

For you mathematicians out there...

Positive Words (your thoughts) +
Uplifted Emotions (your feelings)
= Epic Experience

What Does That Really Mean?

Imagine it like this. You can say the self-talk, "I am great." But if you don't *feel it* with an elevated emotion, like love, joy, or gratitude, then it's not as meaningful or as powerful. The different parts of your brain aren't in coherence, and it doesn't rewire you as fast or draw your manifestations to you with the same power or speed.

Self-talk delivered with low or neutral emotion warrants a grade of B-. It's OK... words alone are surely better than not doing anything at all, but it's nowhere near the A+ level that comes from having the corresponding uplifted emotion. At the top of the class, your results will happen much faster when you get your emotions aligned with the words you're saying.

Note: For some people, only the words will seem possible in the beginning. The emotions will feel too foreign or unrealistic. If that's the case, no problem, just start with the words! Repeat your awesome self-talk over and over, even if you're not feeling it... yet. Because, in time, you will. I promise.

When you say your Coffee Self-Talk accompanied by an uplifted emotion like awe, you feel amazing, and you create a special kind of energy. You feel unlimited. You feel powerful and confident. You feel love. You feel gratitude. These feelings are called *high-frequency energies,* and they attract things with the same frequency—like all the awesome things you imagine for your life. When you say (or read) your Coffee Self-Talk script, and you feel elevated feelings at the same time, then your brain is better able to simulate living in that reality.

In other words, you don't just pay lip service to Coffee Self-Talk. True, you could just repeat the script over and over—with no emotion— and you *will* start to see some changes and feel better eventually. That is a natural consequence of self-talk... your brain will slowly start to rewire itself. But the neural connections will take on Hulk-like proportions, and you'll have tremendously faster success if you pause for a moment with each statement and *feel* what you're saying, in your heart and in your gut, like you *really freakin'* mean it.

Again—because it bears repeating over and over—*it doesn't matter if the affirmation isn't true yet.* The brain doesn't know the difference. It just goes on rewiring itself, and it builds those wires thicker and stronger when there's emotion attached. Emotions are the brain's way of knowing, "this is important; I should pay attention to this." It works the same way with encoding memories. The stronger the emotion, the stronger the memory.

Let's try an example. First, read the following sentence like a robot, with zero emotion:

"I am having the most awesome day today."

Now, close your eyes and imagine what it would actually feel like to have the most awesome day of your life. Really feel it, down to your toes. If necessary, take a few moments to get into this frame of mind. And then, while you're still imagining that level of awesomeness, say with 100% full emotion:

"I am having the most awesome day today!"

Can you feel the difference?

Of course you can! That's your emotions doing their job! *That's* coherence! And think about it—you told your emotions what to do, and they obeyed your command! YOU are in charge. You always are. You only need to use the power you already have over that part of your mind.

Now, whip up some similarly empowered emotions and say, out loud, with passion in your voice:

"I live an amazing life with opportunities all around me. Everything I do is a success. I have success after success."

That would *feel* pretty awesome, right?

Let's unpack this some more. What does awe feel like to you? What does feeling unlimited feel like? Tap into that feeling! If you're still not sure, what would it take to feel awe? Maybe it's witnessing the birth of your child, or watching a sunset from the top of a mountain. Or body surfing in bioluminescent waves, or witnessing the aurora borealis! Do these things fill you with awe? If so, you know the feeling. See the image in your mind as you process each self-talk statement.

Your goal is to feel an elevated emotion while you're saying your Coffee Self-Talk. There are many uplifted emotions from which to choose:

- Love
- Awe
- Inspiration
- Joy
- Bliss
- Generosity
- Abundance
- Limitlessness
- Courage
- Confidence
- Gratitude
- Excitement
- Happiness

... the list goes on and on.

When you experience any of these feelings, you feel elevated. You can tap into any one of them while reading your Coffee Self-Talk. It's not necessary to go through all of them. Any one of those elevated emotions works to uplift your feelings, wire your brain with Hulk wires, and make you feel great.

Another example:

I am healing and healthy right now. I feel whole!

How would it feel to be whole and vibrant? Imagine what it would be like... tap into it... *grab it!* Would you feel energized? Would you feel agile? Virulent? Would you feel strong? Would you feel supple like a leopard? Link those feelings to that statement in your Coffee Self-Talk. Bam! Your thoughts plus your feelings create the *new you*.

Here's a hack to help you increase the feelings and emotions behind the words: Choose *effective words*. Power words. Certain words are cues, or triggers. When chosen carefully, they transform "meh... whatever" into *"holy shit, that's it!"* Again, the emotion you feel will make everything happen much faster. *Feel, to make it real.*

Here are some words that trigger higher emotions. Pick the ones that speak to you. Then, infuse them into your Coffee Self-Talk.

- Aligned
- Amazing
- Awesome
- Beaming
- Blessed
- Blissful
- Bountiful
- Bright
- Calm
- Capable
- Centered
- Clear
- Confident
- Colossal
- Cool
- Creative
- Definitely
- Delighted
- Eager
- Easy
- Ecstatic
- Empower
- First
- Focus

- Freedom
- Funny
- Genuine
- Glowing
- Guaranteed
- Happy
- Helpful
- Honored
- Incredible
- Inspired
- Instantly
- Joyous
- Laughing
- Light
- Lively
- Luminous
- Natural
- Open-minded
- Playful
- Radiant
- Reflective
- Relaxed
- Sensational
- Smiling
- Spirited
- Spontaneous
- Sunny
- Tremendous
- Uplifted
- Vibrant
- Vigorous
- Wondrous

So, you wanna play ball? Amp up the energy with uplifted feelings to turbo charge your Coffee Self-Talk and reach your goals faster. And the longer you're experiencing these elevated emotions and feelings, throughout your whole day, the more you draw opportunities for health, wellness, success, love, and wealth to you. It's time to acknowledge the strength and power within you.

A person is what he or she thinks about all day long.

— RALPH WALDO EMERSON

Chapter 7

THE AUTHOR'S COFFEE SELF-TALK

Before we go any further, I want to share with you my own personal Coffee Self-Talk to really give you an idea of how far I take it.

As I mentioned, it takes me 20 minutes to run through the whole thing (5–10 minutes if I'm in a hurry). I'm a glitzy gal, and I personally resonate with words like glitter, shine, twinkle, rainbow, so you'll see that I frequently use language like that. And saying the statements, digesting them with uplifted emotions and feelings, letting each one sink into my bones, resonate within, and radiate outward like beams of sunshine. It's a beautiful process, and I light up like a Christmas tree. Not a bad way to start the day, eh?

As a dude, your most resonant words might be more masculine. I mean, dudes can sparkle and shine, too, but you might also want a little *grrrr* in your self-talk.

In this book, I don't include pictures or emojis (but I use them a lot, which you'll learn more about in the next chapter). Here, you'll see the words I use. You'll notice there's a lot of repetition. That's deliberate, as repetition is another powerful way to make your brain remember, with more firing and wiring. Sometimes I say the exact same thing the exact same way. Other times, I say things in a new and different way.

To repeat: Repetition is powerful. Use it.

So, without further ado... welcome to my little inner world. Sit back and enjoy.

Kristen's Coffee Self-Talk

Here we go...

I bless everything in my life, right here and right now, with love and appreciation. My life is filled with wonder, awe, and I am powerful. I wake up every day feeling power and happiness coursing through my veins, juicing me up for an incredible day.

I'm worthy, I am strong, and I believe in my abilities to manifest my dreams.

I am forever grateful for my life. I have appreciation for my family, my comfortable bed, my delicious coffee, my shoes, my abundance of money, my wonderful body, my healthy eyes, my strong teeth, my beautiful self, my everything.

I love the power I feel in my life... to design the life I want. The power of feeling good now, no matter what, and I hold the key to the achievement of anything I desire.

What is it I welcome today in my life?

I welcome gratitude. I welcome smiles and winks at myself in the mirror. I welcome love and health and money and abundance. I gratefully receive everything I design because I'm worthy. I have the healthiest body ever.

What is the greatest ideal of myself that I can be today? What new possibilities exist that I will tap into and explore? See the possibilities.

I am in the right place, at the right time, doing the right thing. All is shimmering, glittering, and wonderful in my world.

I am my own hero. There is no one else in the world like me. I am me, and I love me. I'm always learning and growing. I love how I think and feel. I love the power I have to design the life I want.

I have energy and enthusiasm for life! I'm excited! YEEAAHHH BABY!

I'm a born leader and teacher. I think differently. I make different choices. I've crossed the river of change. There's no going back, because I'm a new Kristen. Fly, gorgeous butterfly, fly!

I don't finish a negative thought, statement, or affirmation; I immediately reverse it with uplifting energy, and this feels good every time I do it.

My life is filled with wonder, awe, and I am powerful.

I am calm because I am confident and self-assured. I am worthy of all of my heart's desires. My body is whole and healthy, in every cell from head to toe—inside and out. I am young and beautiful. My body makes gorgeous collagen and my skin is radiant, youthful, and glowing.

The best way to predict my awesome future is to create it from the unknown. With open hands. Here I go!

When I'm already in a state of worthiness, excitement, wholeness, gratitude, joy, love, awe, generosity, and empowerment, then I feel like my desires have already manifested. This connects my current feelings to the ones I know are in the future, and my body believes it's already happened. This connection helps me manifest everything I want faster.

Whatever I am guided to do will be a success. Everything I touch is a success. I go from success to success and have fun the whole time. I deserve the best, and I accept the best now. Money is easy to get!

Money loves me! Money loves me! Money loves me!

I am an excellent steward of money, and I love enjoying it and sharing it with others.

I feel healthy, strong, whole, and vibrant.

I AM Love. Gratitude. Joy. Awe. Excitement. Generosity.

I Feel Empowered. I Feel Bliss.

I Feel Unlimited. I am a Creator.

I lift up others. I give compliments freely to loved ones and strangers alike. A simple compliment can turn someone's day around for the better, especially from a stranger. I put good into the world. I compliment four people every day. I start with Myself. Then someone in my family. Then someone outside my inner circle whom I know, and then also one stranger.

I am compassionate. I am charismatic. I love my new life.

I accept the reality that wealth is mine. **I know my brain is super-powered, and I learn anything I want** *easily, including Italian. I am a creative genius and a prolific writer. I gratefully accept and welcome my AWESOME freedom-filled life!*

"At the center of my being I have the answer; I know who I am, and I know what I want." — The Buddha (rewritten in the first person)

My imagination, aroused emotionally to an intense degree of excitement, plus my confident expectancy, bring an avalanche of fortune to me.

I have an unlimited supply of brilliant ideas, creativity, and sparkling prosperity. I have multiple streams of income. I now receive my good from known and unknown sources! I am capable.

My thankful heart is always close to the riches and creative abundance of the Universe. I am grateful for my beautiful life.

I look at the world around me and feel bright-n-healthy light and energy— a world full of optimism and compassion. I spread joy.

There is so much beauty all around, today and for every tomorrow.

Doors open for me everywhere I turn. *I'm surrounded by opportunities, and I welcome them.*

I am worthy and open to receive. I feel healthy, strong, whole, and vibrant.

When I direct my subconscious mind to believe that health, wealth, and abundance are mine, and they're always circulating in my life, I'll always have them, regardless of the form they take. There is nothing I cannot be, do, or have. I am vibration. I am electricity. I create my future.

Wealth, health, and abundance are mine. *They're always circulating all around me and in my life. I'm worthy. We all are!*

I can do anything. I go after it, and I get it! I'm on top of the world, and I'm going for it! I'm unlimited!

I have an overflowing amount of energy, and I buzz with it. I'm electric. (Bzzt Bzzt Bzzt!)

I have clarity, and I think clearly every day. I love myself.

I'm worthy. I'm worthy. I'm worthy. *I deserve the very best in life.*

I am a genius with an abundance of creative ideas.

I am magnificent. I am lovable. I approve of myself.

The doors between dimensions open to me, so that I may experience the mystical. Synchronicities happen in my life all the time.

My body is full of vitality and strength. *I'm overflowing with uplifting energy, health, and love, and it attracts everything I want in my life. I feel youthful and happy and imagine my genes of youth expressing themselves. Love my self. Always. I am happy and at peace. My body expresses longevity genes.*

I feel loved deeply and daily. I'm worthy of excellence, love, and vitality. I'm whole. I have an abundance of time, energy, and help.

My body feels younger every day. I feel happiness every day. My immune system is powerful and strong.

My healing energy spreads to others.

There is power in me and all around me.

*My mind and brain have an **abundance of focus, and my memory is sharp.***

I rejoice in everyone's prosperity. I love the good fortune of others. And in doing so, I also attract good fortune to myself. We are all connected.

What I am seeking also seeks ME. I am a powerful magnet attracting everything that bestows me with my very own prosperity vibration and electromagnetic frequency. I feel an ocean wave of peace wash over me right now.

I have wings. I feel free, light, calm, patient, rested and relaxed. I am fit, strong, happy, and full of life. I am open to receive.

I believe in my self.

Believe it or not, that's not even all of my daily Coffee Self-Talk. Imagine lots of emojis and powerful images to go along with it (see Chapter 8). The versions morph as I tweak words and add new lines I think about throughout the day.

I also find certain things permanently groove in my brain, and as a result, I no longer need to keep them in the script. They become internalized. Repetition is no longer required. Which means I can replace them with something new.

I also sometimes make changes just to mix things up. Repeating the same things over and over can get boring in any part of life. Making changes, whether adding a picture one day or rearranging words another day, keeps it fresh. When it stays fresh, your brain pays more attention.

Later in this book (Part II), I'll go through many more Coffee Self-Talk scripts for you to start with, or to inspire you to write your own.

But before we dive into that, I'd first like to share another personal story, and then we'll go over a few techniques for turbo-charging your Coffee Self-Talk, taking it to the next level, and infusing it into other parts of your life.

How My Coffee Self-Talk Transformed Me into a Romance Author

I want to share the story of how my Coffee Self-Talk specifically helped my life. When I first began the process, my life started to improve, from day one. I was happier, more energetic and bouncy, and life was easier, more enjoyable. It made me confident, feeling beautiful, and it motivated me to take action on things that I'd written in my scripts about health and wellness.

But I also wrote something else in my scripts. Something that, at the time, I honestly didn't know how it would, or could, come to be. But up until then, self-talk had done wonders for me, so I figured, what the hell, and I gave it a go. What did I have to lose?

I created an entire script about becoming a novelist. I had written a lot of non-fiction, but fiction was a weird and mysterious world to me. I hadn't even read very much of it in recent years. My self-talk related to my ability to create stories was atrocious. I had never thought of myself as a "storyteller." I never thought I had the ability to do it. That was other people—like that loner guy in high school who always carried around a notepad, jotting down ideas. It was not me.

Of course, once I started doing self-talk, I realized that my beliefs about my ability to write fiction were... *a fiction* themselves! Completely made up. Where did they come from? Who knows. Don't care. It was time to change them.

So I started including lines in my daily Coffee Self-Talk script about being a writer. By adding them to a self-talk script that I was already enjoying, and believing it, I was able to sneak in a few lines about a topic that I previously thought I had no talent in *whatsoever*. Hell, I didn't even know where to begin.

I added lines such as:

I am a prolific writer.
I am a creative genius.
I am filled with stories.
Writing novels is easy for me.

That's it. I added several lines like that and went through my routine of reading my Coffee Self-Talk, every morning, day after day.

And what do you know? I'm sitting in my mom's backyard one day when we were stuck in Arizona during self-isolation from the COVID-19 pandemic, and a story idea came to me. Seemingly from nowhere. Out of the blue. *Whoa. Mind blown.* I even looked behind me to see if something had put the idea in my head. Because, like, who me? With a story idea?

From nowhere.

Or... was it?

Question: What is the source of all creativity?

Answer: The subconscious!

Well *of course* I didn't know where the idea came from. That's literally what *subconscious* means.

But where does the subconscious learn that it can generate story ideas?

Answer: From our programming. In this case, my self-talk. It's the only way to explain why it never happened once in the forty-some years of my life prior to doing self-talk related to writing fiction. Not one story idea during that time. NOT ONE.

And then I started telling myself I have lots of story ideas. And suddenly, story ideas started coming to me out of "nowhere."

I was shocked. Even though I believed in the power of self-talk, the speed of my transformation, and the clarity of this event—I must admit—seemed too good to be true. It seemed like *magic*.

But it was not to be a one-off event. It kept happening. And I went down the rabbit hole with that story, and scenes started flowing into my mind!

It happens so regularly now, predictably, that I no longer react with shock. I've come to expect random story ideas hitting me from the ethers. Now, when a story or scene idea hits, I react by saying reinforcing self-talk: *"Yeah, you go, girl. You're a rockstar!"*

So, my self-talk gave me a talent, a skill, that I previously never dreamed I could possess. And although I never speak like that now (words like, "I never thought I could," etc.), I'm repeating them here to relay the story, and it's important to understand my old mindset.

Fast forward six months. As of this writing, I've written six romance novels under the pen name Brisa Starr. That's six novels in five months, which works out to about 6000 words a day during the writing phase (as opposed to editing). And I've got a list of ideas for future novels as long as my arm.

So where did all of this creativity come from, suddenly in my forties, after never having written a single word of fiction in my life?

You already know the answer. The creativity came from my self-talk.

My breakthrough was like opening a floodgate. Once I realized that a story came from my very own brain, it meant "hey, this is actually possible." Like when Roger Bannister broke the 4-minute mile in 1954 —a feat which many people had previously thought impossible— and then someone else broke his record just 46 days later.

In other words, once I knew it was possible, *I knew it was possible.*

A few nights after that first story idea came to me, I couldn't fall asleep. My mind was flooded with story ideas! I want to cry just thinking about this and sharing it with you. I went from thinking I sucked at something, to actually being able to do that something!

All because of my self-talk. I rewired my brain and simply told myself, "I'm a prolific writer. I'm a creative genius." Over, and over, and over. And then it became true.

Well, then I was on a roll. I created an entire *Writer's Self-Talk* script. I wrote it down on a big index card, and I recorded myself reading it with groovy background music. I listened to it almost every day. I still do, many months later.

My Writer's Coffee Self-Talk Script

I am a prolific writer. I write 10 books a year.

I love my brain. It's strong, healthy, and full of power.

I am resilient.

I'm a beautiful and creative genius.

I am filled with stories.

I am brave.

I am so excited to wake up every morning, so that I can write my novels.

I love my life, and life loves me.

I am focused.

I live in a higher level of mind.

My heart is filled with joy and excitement.

My brain is filled with AWE.

I am defined by the vision of my best-selling author future.

Words and scenes for novels are pouring out of me.

I love my life. And I love my stories.

I'm having so much fun writing fiction.

Writing novels is in my blood.

I'm a best-selling author.

I write five to seven thousand words a day.

Watch Me Go!

I'm a Happy Sexy Millionaire.

I'm an incredible writer.

Writing is exciting. I'm a storyteller.

Writing novels is easy and fun for me.

I easily dictate books with my digital voice recorder.

I bless my laptop with love. It brings me money every day.

I love me. All is incredibly well.

That is the original script, and as I typed it here for you to read, I was reading it off the giant index card it's written on, which sits on my desk.

I'll soon make it more specific because I have a new goal: to write fantasy novels. I currently write steamy romance novels, and I love writing them, but decided I wanted to branch out into other genres.

But guess what?

Remember, I don't really say the following to myself, but negative programming tried to creep in...

"But, Kristen, you know nothing about writing fantasy. How in the hell will you create those epic worlds and characters and storylines? With wars, fairies, monsters, and magic shit?"

Mwahaha!—I laugh in the face of those wimpy thoughts that dare to enter my head.

Of course I can write fantasy! It's simply a matter of priming myself to do it. I don't know when it'll manifest, but I certainly know how to begin the process... with my Coffee Self-Talk. So, in the *Writer's Self-Talk* script above, I'll add lines like:

I'm a best-selling fantasy author.

Words and scenes for fantasy novels are pouring out of me.

I create epic, magical, mind-blowing fantasy worlds!

It's that simple.

Chapter 8

TURBO-CHARGED COFFEE SELF-TALK

Now that you're familiar with the basics of Coffee Self-Talk, it's time to see how far you can take this rocket ship to the future of your own design. Let's take things to the next level with ways to use Coffee Self-Talk that will enhance the experience even more.

I regularly do all of the following for maximum energy, power, and epic living.

1. Use Images

Our brains adore images.

You can make your Coffee Self-Talk more powerful by adding pictures to your self-talk scripts. When you do this, it gets more parts of your brain firing, which helps you feel the elevated emotions even more.

Images are more memorable than words, which is why memory experts say the key to remembering things easily is to incorporate images when learning or memorizing anything. Images will cause you to remember your self-talk more easily throughout the day as the images get burned into your mind. You can do this with pictures from the Internet, pictures you take yourself, or even pencil-and-paper sketches or doodles. Think of it as "Coffee Self-Talk Meets Vision Board." Images turbo-boost your brain's rewiring process.

You can use images with every statement if you like, or only occasionally, for special emphasis. The pictures can relate directly to the statement, but they don't have to. What's most important is that the picture triggers the uplifted emotion you're trying to capture.

For example, for the script, *I am having the most awesome day today!*, you could add a picture right after that statement. Just grab any stock photo you love from the Internet. It could be a picture of the ocean, or the mountains, an animal, or art. Anything that inspires awe in you.

My own Coffee Self-Talk has lots of pictures I grab from the Internet to inspire me. When I see them, I feel extra power coursing through my veins. The pictures make me feel more electric and amplify my feelings. For example, I have a part of my script where I write about my new self. It says:

> *I am a new person. I look into my eyes and see what others see. I gave up the old identity, and I'm living a completely new, magical life of my design. Courageous. Excited. In Awe. In Love with Life. Patient. Kind. Shimmering Gold.*

Then, following the statement is a picture of the phoenix bird burning, transforming, and rising from the ashes.

For wanting to feel healthy and whole, you would add a picture of something that makes you *feel* healthy and whole. Maybe it's a picture of healthy food. Or athletes. Or running on the beach with a dog. Or maybe it's an amazing log cabin in the woods with mountains all around. Add those pictures throughout your Coffee Self-Talk to inspire and boost those uplifted feelings.

The experience of seeing these images while doing your Coffee Self-Talk is like reviewing a living, breathing, powered-up vision board. When you add pictures and emphasis to your self-talk, and read it aloud while seeing these pictures, the realization of your legendary life can happen faster. You can practically feel it happening in real time.

2. Emojis

Another fun and quick way to enhance your Coffee Self-Talk is with emojis. My pages of scripts are filled with them: smiles, sun, moon, stars, fireworks, lightning, explosion, bicep, coffee (of course), the bag of money, airplane, sailboat, beach/island, and more. Get creative. It's a fun and meaningful process, and you'll find yourself adding to it over time. There's something about the lighthearted playfulness of the designs that engages you at a subtle emotional level, which is what we're going for.

3. Fonts, Underlines, Italics, and Bold

To add emphasis to certain phrases, I underline words, bold, and/or italicize them. I center-align certain statements, right-justify others, and change the spacing of the words to add visual variety. I use my iPhone's Notes app to enter my own little scribble drawings, too. All of these make your self-talk more emotionally resonant, attention-grabbing, and just plain fun.

4. Optimize Your Coffee Self-Talk Environment

Environment can make or break your Coffee Self-Talk experience. It's best done in a physical space that's comfortable and inspiring, yet allows you to have good posture. No slouching! According to research, sitting straight with good posture can increase energy and reduce stress, making you feel happier. That said, if you get especially happy relaxing into, say, a big comfy couch, then I say, hey, do whatever heightens your bliss.

Look around your kitchen, office, or living room, and see what looks good. If you don't have a place that jumps out at you, take the opportunity to organize a space for this intended purpose. I typically do my Coffee Self-Talk in a sitting area in our kitchen, and sometimes I do it on the couch in the living room. When I visit my mom in Arizona, I do it outside, in the morning, under the always bright, blue sky on her patio (this is one of my favorite places for Coffee Self-Talk).

When you're intentional about your environment, you can shape it to amplify your experience, emotions, and feelings. That's super important for your Coffee Self-Talk time because it makes the entire process more intentional. Which, in turn, makes it more powerful and effective. You want to love the space you're in, because it'll boost your mood and keep you motivated to stick to your habit every day. Using the same space every time will also trigger your optimal state, just like the coffee does.

That said, if you can't use the same ideal place every day, don't worry about it. Just do it wherever you can.

Many other factors contribute to the totality of your environment when doing Coffee Self-Talk. Your preferences may vary, but I generally feel most empowered and uplifted in a spa-like environment. Not because I like spas per se (which I do), but because spas have, through decades of trial and error, perfected environments for making people feel relaxed. Here are some things to consider for enhancing your environment:

- **Natural sunlight**—especially nice, as Coffee Self-Talk is usually a morning ritual. Sunlight will help you wake up, get focused, and put you in a good mood.
- **Nature of any sort**—an outdoor setting, fresh air, breeze, plants.
- **Water features**—nothing beats the sound of a babbling

brook for tapping into your inner juju. Even a desktop fountain works wonders for the soul (all day long, too, not just during your Coffee Self-Talk). In fact, according to marine biologist, Wallace J. Nichols, author of *Blue Mind*, the term "blue mind" refers to a mildly meditative state that people fall into when near, in, on, or under water.

- **Emotion-inducing aromas**—coffee(!), bacon, fresh baked bread, incense, a fire in the fireplace... whatever you prefer. One reader reports doing his self-talk in his sports car before work every morning because his leather seats "smell like success"... lol—like I said, whatever works. As *Apocalypse Now*'s Lt. Colonel Kilgore said in one of the most famous movie quotes of all time, "I love the smell of napalm in the morning... it smells like victory." Despite this legendary line's perverse irony, you have to give its writer credit for capturing something magical in just a few words. Smell is perhaps the world's most underutilized power tool for hacking your brain, so be sure to put it to good use.
- **Sounds**—water (again), wind chimes, birds, music (more on this one, below)
- **Freedom from distractions**—turn off the TV, put your phone in airplane mode, tell everyone in your house to leave you alone.

5. Say It Out Loud

Some people choose to read their self-talk silently to themselves. Sometimes this might be your only option, such as in a crowded public space. That said, whenever possible, say your self-talk out loud!

When you speak your self-talk out loud, you'll be more focused, and your mind will be less likely to wander. It also uses three modalities: reading (eyes), speaking (mouth), and hearing (ears). Which means it's roughly three times as powerful as reading silently, with respect to the level of activity inside your brain.

Oftentimes, when reading silently, your mind can wander. Such as thinking about your to-do list, or thinking about how you slept the night before, or a phone call you have to make at work. By reading, speaking, and hearing your self-talk, it makes your focus laser-sharp. This, in turn, makes the words easier to remember, and it makes them more meaningful, too. Speaking the words also makes them enter your subconscious mind for faster effectiveness, and it helps you connect with a deeper emotional response.

As I've said many times already, it's OK if you don't yet believe the words coming out of your mouth. You can totally *fake it till you make it* because that actually works. Muhammad Ali was famous for doing this. He once said, "To be a great champion, you must believe you are the best. If you're not, pretend you are."

Even when you're pretending, you're still firing and wiring, because your brain doesn't know the difference between what you're imagining is happening and what is really happening. You can think of it as "rehearsing for success." Pretty soon, you won't be pretending.

You might be skeptical about the claim that your brain doesn't know the difference between what you say and what is true. I mean, part of you knows the difference... the part of you that's doing the talking, of course. But the part of your brain that's wiring new neural connections—it doesn't know the difference. It's just connecting neurons. This is why, for instance, people can increase their blood pressure and release cortisol, just with their thoughts. You can tell yourself you're happy over and over, filling your head with thoughts and visions of happy encounters, and your brain will believe you're happy.

And if you can't say your self-talk out loud for whatever reason, at a minimum, mouthing the words silently will have more impact than just reading your Coffee Self-Talk to yourself. At a VERY minimum, have good posture while you're doing this. Trust me on this, it just works. Something about snapping to *attention* and mouthing the words with *intention*—makes your brain take notice. (Do a little experiment right now and try this. You'll see what I mean!)

6. Add Energy to Your Coffee Self-Talk

For even more impact, get really animated during your Coffee Self-Talk. By really emphasizing the words and whooping-n-hollering between statements—*YEAHHH!!!*—you amplify your emotional state.

The more action and emphasis you put into this, the better and more believable it will be for your mind and body. So go for the gusto! Tap into your inner Cuba Gooding Jr. Act it, man! By really getting into it, you carve those affirming self-talk grooves deeper into your brain, and faster.

Your body *will* respond to your words. And if you add bravado, energy, and intensity, the response will be even stronger.

Even better is to sometimes stand up and say your self-talk in a power pose, like Thor. Yes, that's right. Or Captain America. Power poses have actually been shown to increase confidence and decrease stress, so take advantage of them. Feel silly doing it? No problem, do it anyway. Make a joke of it, if you like. Ham it up. Here's a good one: hands on hips, eyes straight ahead, and a slight, knowing smile. (You know the one, that knowing smile that shows you have the secrets, the power, and the answers.) *Yes! Power up, people!*

7. Make It Like a Movie by Adding a Soundtrack

Without music, life would be a mistake.

— FRIEDRICH NIETZSCHE

The next level in Coffee Self-Talk badassery comes when you add powerful music to the mix. It can be playing in the background as you read your self-talk out loud, or mixed into self-talk you record yourself or purchase.

Adding music while reading your Coffee Self-Talk will amplify and intensify the feelings you want to create. Music can evoke powerful emotional responses, and it's one of the best and easiest ways to reduce stress, alter your mood, and change your state. It's believed that pleasurable music can trigger the release of the neurotransmitter dopamine, which is known as the "reward" neurotransmitter. You can therefore train yourself to *want* to do your Coffee Self-Talk by combining it with pleasurable music, because you'll secrete dopamine every time you hear it, and your brain will start to associate doing your Coffee Self-Talk with receiving that reward.

I've mentioned the importance of feelings while reading your Coffee Self-Talk, and an easy way to uplift your emotional state is by listening to uplifting music while you're going through it. There's a reason movies have soundtracks and scores. They drive people's emotions while watching the movies. Imagine one of your favorite dramas or action-packed summer blockbusters, and think about what it would be like without music! The experience would be so much less moving or memorable. By adding uplifting music, you'll not only take your Coffee Self-Talk to the next level, but you'll also enjoy it more!

The music you play affects your brain. Scientists don't yet know exactly why this is, but it appears that part of the reason music is so powerful is that it engages many parts of the brain, triggering connections and creating associations. If you repeatedly listen to the same song while reading (or singing!) your Coffee Self-Talk, you will anchor the music to the words. Then, whenever you hear that song, your head will fill with your powerful Coffee Self-Talk. (More precisely, the mental state encoded with the self-talk will get loaded into your brain.)

Go through your favorite songs, and find one that uplifts your spirit, inspires your soul, and moves you emotionally to feel powerful and energized. Then, put it on repeat and listen to it while you read your Coffee Self-Talk. Call it your "Coffee Self-Talk song." Or you could compile several songs and create a "Coffee Self-Talk playlist." I like the playlist idea for its variety, but I personally find that repeating just one song, over and over, is most powerful because it anchors that one song very strongly. In a few months, or even a year, I might move on to a different song, or when entering a new chapter in life.

Pro-tip: Choose a song *without lyrics* so the words don't compete with your focus as you read your Coffee Self-Talk. I find certain movie scores have the perfect epic, dramatic, cinematic feel for this purpose.

Another interesting aspect of combining music with your Coffee Self-Talk is that it's a powerful emotional stimulus that can change your relationship with time. Have you ever noticed how time flies when you're listening to something you like, or how time stands still, like you momentarily transport to a different reality, and then return to this reality when the music ends? Or how music can put you into a timeless, almost hypnotic trance?

Neuroscientists and artists have been putting their brains into alpha wave states (8–12 Hz) for decades to achieve relaxation, visualization, creativity, and enhanced learning. As have meditators, for thousands of years. My intuition and personal experience tell me that some-thing powerful is happening when entering this type of altered state and reading my self-talk. It's also very pleasant, and therefore makes you more likely to do it every day.

I've recently anchored the song, *Liquid Flow*, by Dreaming Cooper (you can find it on YouTube) as the theme song for my daily Coffee Self-Talk. It's got a futuristic, electronic, ambient vibe, with no real melody. That is, it's music that creates a powerful, distinctive mood but doesn't attempt to tell any kind of story. Which is exactly what I want. Now, whenever I hear that music, I'm instantly programmed to think and feel everything I've drilled into my brain by doing my Coffee Self-Talk. It's awesome!

And how often does that particular piece of music come up in my day?

Exactly five.

Why five? This takes me to the next tip... my *Millionaire Minute*.

8. My Millionaire Minute

I have devised a powerful technique I call my *Millionaire Minute*. It's an alarm on my cell phone that plays a specific piece of music at certain times of the day, and it serves to trigger my Happy Sexy Millionaire *state*. That is, the thoughts, feelings, and general mindset I've associated with manifesting my Happy Sexy Millionaire self.

It's an amazing state of mind, and I live in it all day long—kinda sorta —as some moments are stronger than others. Sometimes, the mundane details of existence, like doing laundry, paying bills, or buying groceries cause me to momentarily forget about my epic, shiny, golden mission.

And then, all of the sudden, my Millionaire Minute alarm goes off!

And... *BAM!!*

When I hear the opening notes of the music, I'm instantly transported into that mental space where all the magic happens.

I immediately stop whatever I'm doing (except when impossible or inappropriate), close my eyes, sit up (or stand) straight, take a deep breath, and simply let the feeling wash over me. It's amazing, and never fails to get me right back on track if I had become distracted by unimportant things. I remain frozen in this mild trance-like state for anywhere from 10–60 seconds. Then, I stop the alarm and resume my day, but with a completely refreshed outlook and elevated emotions.

And this happens *five times a day!*

I've set the alarm on my phone to go off every day at 10:00 a.m., 12:00 p.m., 2:00 p.m., 4:00 p.m., and 6:00 p.m. It's programmed to play *Liquid Flow* by Dreaming Cooper at those designated times.

What does this do? Well, as I mentioned earlier, I've anchored that particular song to feeling awesome, as a result of always listening to it while I read my Coffee Self-Talk. When the alarm goes off, I'm reminded of my powerful Coffee Self-Talk that makes me feel like a million bucks. It reminds me that I'm manifesting that every day. Not just with positive thoughts, but with every action I take, and the effort and love I put into my work. This reminder sets my brain to feeling good and uplifted. It taps me into the life I'm manifesting with my Coffee Self-Talk.

My family knows all about my Millionaire Minute ritual. In fact, now, when that alarm goes off, my whole family actually joins me in letting the music surround us as we feel shimmery-golden good. My husband isn't always in the same room with me and my phone when it happens, so he might only hear it 2–3 times a day. Even though he hasn't linked *Liquid Flow* to self-talk, he says the music "resets" him and never fails to produce a more focused, empowered mental state. It serves as a frequent reminder to live day-to-day life at an epic level.

9. Record Your Coffee Self-Talk

Next up for the superstars is to record your self-talk... *wait for it...* with your chosen song playing in the background! OMG, it's totally cool and fascinating. By recording your self-talk, you can now listen to it at any time. Like walking to the store, driving in the car, getting ready in the morning, working out at the gym, mowing the lawn, or before bed as you're going to sleep.

Heck, one of my ultimate favorite ways to do my Coffee Self-Talk is with my coffee mug in hand, while walking around my kitchen and living room, with my headphones on, listening to my recorded self speaking into my ears. It's a triple habit stack:

Coffee + Self-Talk + Walking

There's some potentially powerful stuff going on here, making your self-talk more effective.

For starters, the repetitive motion that occurs while walking triggers an almost immediate relaxation response in your body. When this happens, my stress instantly starts to dissipate. Simultaneously, we get a boost in energy to accompany our uplifted mood.

Remember, uplifted feelings and elevated emotions are key ingredients to making your self-talk and dreams materialize faster. The bilateral motion of walking benefits our brains in remarkable ways. Plus? You get in some extra steps for the day! And if you want even more intensity, you can do what I sometimes do: drink coffee, listen to and speak Coffee Self-Talk, while... doing walking lunges!

I understand we don't all have time to regularly sit down and read our Coffee Self-Talk every single morning. By recording it, you can listen to it and tap into its greatness on days when you're rushed and drinking your coffee on the go. Or, if you're going all out, it means you can experience your life-changing self-talk more than once a day. Sit down with your Coffee Self-Talk, as normal, by reading it and sipping coffee in the morning. Then, when you're making dinner or doing the dishes, play it again in the background.

Hearing your own recorded voice can be a little weird at first. That's normal, and it's always temporary. Like the strangeness of seeing yourself in the mirror with a new haircut—what seems so unfamiliar at first quickly becomes something you don't even notice. It's the same with hearing your own voice. It's worth going through this adjustment period, because the impact of hearing your own self-talk is super powerful!

When you hear your own voice—especially once you're used to hearing it, and not judging it—it plays like an internal dialog in your mind. Like "you" telling "you" how things are. And when you think about it, this is exactly what happens when we think! We think in dialog—mostly unspoken—with ourselves constantly. "What should I wear today? Hmm, I like this shirt, but I wore it two days ago..." etc.

Our minds are made up of several systems, each with its own "personality." For instance, the "rational" brain vs. the "feeling" brain, etc. Or the part of you that wants to lose 10 pounds, versus the part of you that thinks just one more slice of pizza won't hurt. I like to think of my recorded self-talk as my "higher self"—the part of my brain that knows what's best for me in the long run—and I trust it. When I hear this voice, it has a kind of authority. It's a kind of power, and it comes from me!

Coffee Self-Talk is especially helpful in trying times. In fact, I was editing this book during the coronavirus pandemic of 2020, and I relied heavily on my recorded Coffee Self-Talk to keep me uplifted, healthy, and empowered amid the constant fear and news. If I felt overwhelmed at any moment, my favorite thing to do was put in my wireless earbuds and have my recorded Coffee Self-Talk playing in the background while I cleaned, worked, cooked, exercised, and walked around the house.

Here's how I go about recording my own self-talk:

There's nothing fancy here... no professional audio equipment or anything like that. I'm the only one who's going to hear it, and it doesn't have to be perfect.

As I mentioned, I use the Notes app on my iPhone to type my Coffee Self-Talk. This is very convenient, as my phone is always on me, and so I can add to my self-talk script and make edits any time I get an idea, or the inspiration hits me. I also have an iPad, which syncs with that Note in the cloud. So I pull up my Coffee Self-Talk on the iPad and read it from there. I also have that *Liquid Flow* music playing on my iPad while I'm reading. Then, I open the Voice Memo application that comes pre-installed on the iPhone, though any recording app would work.

I then record my Coffee Self-Talk into my iPhone, while reading it out loud from the iPad, with the music playing in the background on the iPad. The end result blends my voice with the music just fine. This process won't win any Oscars for its sound quality, but it's more than good enough to reprogram your brain for living your legendary life!

If you don't have a separate tablet to read from, just read your self-talk script from your computer, or print it out on paper. And the music isn't necessary, but it's more effective. It's also more fun!

Or, you could always just write your script down on paper, and read from that while you record. This doesn't need to be complicated, and you shouldn't let your desire to make it perfect cause you to delay doing it. You can always improve things later.

On most days, I listen to my recorded self-talk once a day. Sometimes, I'm feeling extra energized, and I leave it playing on an endless loop for much of the day, listening on headphones while I go about my business. It's amazing!

10. Coffee Self-Talk Calendar Reminder

It's easy to get lost in the day. It's easy to get lazy and forgetful when we're busy and distracted. One tip to counteract this is to take one line from your Coffee Self-Talk and simply copy and paste the written text into your phone's calendar. Set it to show up every day. Then, every day, when you're busy living life, you'll suddenly see self-talk on your calendar. It's a little reminder of your awesomeness. This is really effective, and yet so simple.

We all get distracted with day-to-day life, and we sometimes forget to think about the big picture, our goals and aspirations. Or, even if we remember the goals, we forget to be *always moving towards them*. Or sometimes, our emotions rule us, instead of the other way around. We forget to feel good, and we need reminders that it's possible to feel good all the time, or at least 95% of the time. Self-talk reminders are perfect for this.

Sometimes I set the following self-talk as my daily reminder:

I am a kind and thoughtful mom.

You'd think a mom wouldn't need to be reminded of this, but, well, I find it helps me to be reminded of such things. When I see this, it reminds me to give my undivided attention to my daughter when she asks me something or to give her extra snuggles.

On another day, I'll change it to:

I am powerful and charismatic.

I tell ya... just seeing this gives me an edge in that moment. My behavior instantly changes.

The trick with these reminders is to choose short, snappy sentences. You want the whole thing to show up in your calendar, which displays a limited number of characters. When you find a sentence that really resonates with you, keep using it for a while. Sometimes I set the same one to repeat for two weeks, eventually making its way into my subconscious, and I never need reminding. And then I switch it to something new.

Other times, I choose one snippet per day and simply hit "weekly" repeat, so I'm rotating through seven different phrases each week. I can't emphasize enough how effective this little tip is.

11. Coffee Self-Talk Sticky Reminders

Next up: the old-fashioned *Post-it Note*. I mentioned this in Chapter 1, and it's the analog version of the calendar reminder, above. Writing out some of your favorite Coffee Self-Talk lines on Post-it Notes, and sticking them in places where you'll see them, helps remind you to stay the course with your positive affirmations. I even read about someone printing out a positive affirmation, laminating it, and hanging it in the shower. What a great idea!

There's another trick to this one though. You have to move the Post-it Notes around every 4–5 days. Otherwise, you become "blind" to them and ignore them. To prevent this, move them to different parts of your home or office, as well as changing the script on them every week or two.

12. The "I am" Mobile App

I recently discovered a new app for iPhone/Android that's perfect for using with your daily Coffee Self-Talk. The app is called "I am," and it's billed as "daily affirmations for self-care," by the app developer, Monkey Taps.

The app has a free preview mode where you can enjoy a few select, preloaded affirmations. The full version costs about $20 a year and gives you access to its full library of pre-loaded affirmations, including a feature that lets you add your own (including emojis, yay!).

And this is where your Coffee Self-Talk comes into play.

Simply add lines from your Coffee Self-Talk script into the application. Click on "Practice," select "My Own Affirmations," and choose a time (one, five, or 15 minutes). The app will randomly display each of your Coffee Self-Talk lines, at 15-second intervals, with colorful backgrounds.

So in this way, it creates a timed Coffee Self-Talk session for you, and another cool way to go through your script!

In addition to using the app during your morning Coffee Self-Talk routine, it's also a great way to fill idle time. Just imagine... standing in line at the grocery store, and you pull out your phone, and the following line from your script appears:

A thankful heart is always close to the riches of the Universe.
I am grateful for my beautiful life.

It's great fun, and the element of randomness adds some excitement to the mix. You never know what you'll see next.

Chapter 9

FINDING TIME TO DO YOUR
COFFEE SELF-TALK

Everybody has time for Coffee Self-Talk. The time it takes to drink a cup of coffee is perfect, and I'll venture to guess every one of us eats or drinks something in the morning, even if it's just a glass of water. Now, if you're the person who drinks your coffee on the go, well, then it's time to make a change, *because you're worth it.*

The question is simply, do you want to feel amazing or not? Do you want to increase your happiness and well-being? Do you want to improve your health and attract a mate or new friends? Do you want to see more opportunities? Do you want to be more successful at work? Do you want to be a better parent? If you answered *yes* to any of these, then five minutes is all you need to get started.

I know there are people who still say they don't have time, but it's super simple. I have the answer for you, the secret to how you can make time to do this. Are you ready?

Wake up 10 minutes earlier.

Magic, I know.

I say this a bit sarcastically, but totally cushioned in love. I want everyone to have incredible self-talk because—it's not an overstatement—the world will truly be a better place. Every individual who improves his or her inner dialog is a butterfly precursor to a hurricane of love, peace, and compassion felt around the world. When we tie our self-talk time to our morning coffee, we're more likely to do it, and it's my dream that everyone starts doing this. Loving themselves, and living lives filled with intention and self-belief.

Yes, it might mean waking a bit earlier, if necessary. And that means going to bed 10 minutes earlier, because I don't want people losing sleep. A good night's sleep is super important for health. It can also alter your mood and upgrade your happiness and zest for life. So, as a side note to rearranging your schedule for Coffee Self-Talk, do yourself and your life a favor... get a good night's rest.

I repeat, we all have the time for this. The fascinating thing is how difficult it can be for people to get to bed just a few minutes earlier. I completely understand. There are many times I'm reading, and I want to finish the chapter. Just five more minutes. Or I'm playing *Words with Friends,* and I want to play my turn on all the games I have going with various people. Just a few more minutes won't hurt, right? Or I'm watching my favorite show on Netflix, and the episode is not quite done. Umm, not gonna hit *pause* in the middle of the chase scene!

And therein lies the secret. To prevent this problem, look at your life to see what you're doing in the evening, in the hour before bed, and make changes. Adjust your schedule to avoid disrupting your evening activities and still get to bed on time. When I looked at my own schedule and evening routine, I found all kinds of excuses to cut into my sleep. And this is where you can find room for improvement.

Simply look at your calendar and use it to help organize your bedtime routine. Once again, I use the calendar app on my iPhone. I plug in the time I want to go to bed each night, which is typically 9:00 p.m. Getting to sleep by 9:00 p.m. gives me plenty of time for sleep, ensuring I wake refreshed, 8–9 hours later. I then set an alarm on my phone for 8:35 p.m., and I choose a sleep-inducing song from the *Soni-caid Sleep Therapy* album to play as the alarm. When it goes off, I stop whatever I'm doing—with almost no exceptions—and I brush my teeth, wash my face, and get into bed. This leaves me a few minutes to review my positive affirmations for the day, before I drift off to sleep.

If this seems basic, that's because *it is!* This is not rocket science. But how many people actually set an alarm to get ready for bed? It's SO easy. And when I know my cut-off time is 8:35 p.m., I don't dare start a show at 8:00 p.m. I've also become accustomed to stopping my reading in the middle of a chapter. I put off playing the rest of my *Words with Friends* games until the next evening.

When I'm traveling or have a hectic schedule, I adjust by going back to my calendar and simply working backwards from the time I want to go to sleep, ensuring I get my 8 hours of sleep *and* time for Coffee Self-Talk in the morning.

The reality is, you don't NOT have time for self-talk. At least, not if you want the epic life that's waiting for you. Besides, seeing that the average person spends over two hours a day on social media, I know most people have 10 minutes to create a better life.

It's simply a matter of deciding, is this a priority or not? For me, it most definitely is. I've experienced life with Coffee Self-Talk and life without it. It's much better with it!

> *Change requires daily, positive habits and routines designed to keep you in alignment with your goals.*
>
> — Dr. Joe Dispenza

Chapter 10

ALTERNATIVE PERSPECTIVE TECHNIQUES (APT)

There are two ways that have made Coffee Self-Talk tremendously helpful in other parts of my life. I call these *Alternative Perspective Techniques,* or APT. Specifically, Coffee Self-Talk has helped me do things I didn't previously like doing. In this chapter, I'll teach you how to use Coffee Self-Talk to help reframe things for the better.

APT #1: Coffee Self-Talk Reframing

Finding a Way to Like What You Don't Want to Do

A sneaky and cool way to use Coffee Self-Talk is to reframe your mind about things you need to do, but you don't really want to. This is one of my favorite ways to use self-talk. When I discovered how powerful the words we use are in determining how we feel and what we manifest, I experimented one day with using different words in an attempt to get me excited to do something I actually didn't want to do.

Even before the words came out of my mouth, I was very skeptical, and I didn't think it would work. I mean, come on, take something I totally don't want to do, and simply change a word, and see if it will make me want to do it? I gave the idea my fiercest stink-eye, but then I thought, *what the hell?*

The first time I tried this technique came one day when I had to pay bills. Which was not something I enjoyed doing. But this time, I tried something different. I simply said, "I love paying bills. I'm happy to do it."

And that was it.

I honest-to-god had an immediate shift in my heart and state. I didn't feel anxiety. With that simple change of words and reframing, in that moment, I was literally happy to pay bills. It seemed too good to be true, but oh man, I ran with it.

By telling myself, *I love paying bills*, my mind listened and created that state for me. It was freakin' magic. After that, I started using this trick all the time. I remember laughing when it worked so easily, and I thought, "Yeah, but will this work for other people, or am I, like, just super weird?"

But then, a few weeks later, I was reading Gretchen Rubin's book, *The Happiness Project*, and she described doing the *exact same thing*. I almost fell off my chair! Hello, fellow fan-girl!

After that first successful experiment, I started using it for everything, and I mean *everything*. If there was something I wasn't stoked about doing, I just told myself that I was totally excited about it. At a minimum, this little mental hack took the sting out of doing it. But most often, I actually started looking forward to the activity.

For example, when I need to run an errand, like going to the store, when there are other things I'd rather be doing, I just change my thoughts. Now I say, "I love going to the store." And off I go, in a better mindset, skipping instead of trudging.

I also use this technique when cleaning our apartment in Italy, especially the oven, which I had always disliked doing. I started telling myself "I love it." I don't even bother coming up with a reason why, because I believe whatever I tell myself. Since the brain takes orders, and I was telling it I loved something, my brain responded with, "Sure, why not?"

This trick works extremely well with exercising, too. So many people don't like working out, and some people, my mom included, routinely describe it with a four-letter word—and I don't mean *love*! But when you start saying "I love exercise!" every time you're about to do it, you actually find yourself enjoying it. Holy moly, *it totally works!*

Turns out, the trick works on how you feel about people, too. I have this one relative I don't always resonate with. I started telling myself that I loved her, and—honest-to-goodness—my energy shifted, and I began to feel more kindness toward her in my heart. And, I'll be damned, I found myself looking forward to spending time with her. And when I did, it was so much more pleasant than before. I imagine she sensed something was different, which seemed to change her energy toward me, as well. It's as though my words had been a self-fulfilling prophecy.

Which is exactly the point of self-talk!

I also tried using this Alternative Perspective Technique for my work. While blogging about becoming a Happy Sexy Millionaire, I considered making YouTube videos. Unfortunately, I didn't really enjoy making videos. I'd always found the process to be stressful: speaking in front of a camera, remembering what I'm supposed to say, finding something to wear, doing my hair, and not screwing up.

So, one day, I experimented with my new APT powers, and I said, "I love making YouTube videos." Well, OMFG, it worked *again*. Game over—checkmate. I now love making videos. And I really do. I'm not faking it. I'm not lying to myself. I now actually get excited thinking about being in front of the camera. I'm more relaxed and better at it now. It's like a switch just flipped in my brain.

I'm still amazed at this technique's simplicity. Maybe I'm a highly suggestible person, but I challenge anyone to repeatedly say you like something that you thought you didn't like, and see if your attitude about it shifts even a little. If it does, it's worth it. The technique can be used for things you only mildly dislike—like cleaning the house or folding laundry—or for things you *reeeally* don't like doing—like public speaking, filing your taxes, or visiting your in-laws!

Fun experiment: Try using it to start liking something *sensory* that you currently don't like, such as a type of food, or genre of music or film. Imagine the possibilities!

This amazing tactic could be super effective for people professionally. Imagine if you were in sales, but you didn't relish cold-calling. By simply telling yourself, "I absolutely love cold calling," you'll shift your attitude and give yourself an edge with a boost of confidence. When you think of the implications for this when applying it to repetitive tasks, it becomes game-changing. The more often you can shift your mind into positive territory, the better you'll feel, the healthier your body will be, and the more legendary your life will become.

For some time now, I've done this anytime something comes up that I normally don't want to do, like flying across the Atlantic, or going through airport security. There's nothing I won't apply it to... cleaning the floors, hanging laundry, going to the DMV. It works like a charm. I'm now working on trying to enjoy the taste of liver—so nutritious, but... ugghh. Progress has been a bit slow, but I can now at least tolerate it thanks to APT.

Try it yourself. Think of something you need to do this week that you'd rather not do. Simply say out loud, "I love doing _____." See if it doesn't instantly make you feel different about the task. If it doesn't, or if the effect is small, then say it over and over, 5–10 times. Then enjoy the instant lift you experience about the upcoming project or to-do item on your list.

While Alternative Perspective Techniques like this don't require coffee, they are a form of self-talk. So, you can use it in your Coffee

Self-Talk. By adding the statements into your Coffee Self-Talk script, you repeat the positive thought on a daily basis, making the change become permanent faster.

For example, paying bills is a monthly recurring to-do item. If every month you feel anxiety when it's bill-pay time, add a line or two to your Coffee Self-Talk script, such as, "I love paying my bills." Saying this every day for a couple of weeks will take the suck out of paying bills. It's actually reprogramming your mind to feel completely different about it.

Almost anything can be seen from different points of view. Not everyone dislikes paying bills. Many people are indifferent toward it; others actually enjoy checking each bill off their list. These are data points that prove it's possible to like something that you don't like. What is perhaps less clear to people, is that liking or disliking something is actually a choice. I *decided* to like paying my bills. And we all have this power to choose our preferences.

You see, it's not the activity itself we dislike, but the way we view it. How we think about things makes the difference. What they *mean* to us. By speaking just a few words of self-talk, you can completely change what something means to you. Be it an activity, a person, or your beliefs about the world. And most of all, your beliefs about *you*. That's empowering!

APT #2: The Game-Changing "GET TO" Alternative Perspective Technique

Another way to reframe things that you "should" do, or have to do, but you don't always like doing, is to change your self-talk language about it in another specific way. Simply replace "have to" with "get to," and then sit back and feel the magic. Here's my favorite example:

Instead of "I *have to* exercise now," say, "I *get to* exercise now."

Bam! Wow! See the difference?

I've changed something that was a "need to do," or a "should do," into a *privilege*. Like, how lucky am I? I get to exercise! Woohoo! By turning it into a privilege, a feeling of gratitude washes over you and makes you much happier about doing the activity.

Changing one little word completely shifts the meaning. Without saying it outright, the implication is that not everyone gets to exercise. Such as if they're working three jobs, or physically impaired. Or, sometimes I *don't* "get to exercise," like when I'm sick. The mere fact that nothing is currently preventing me from physically exerting myself, and improving my physical condition, is reason enough to be happy. It really *is* a privilege.

For those of you who don't love meditating, try telling yourself, "I *get to* meditate today." It makes you feel a bit like a kid.

Do you see how powerful your words are? I use this hack all the time; in fact, every day. Over time, your feelings really do change. You'll become much more excited about the thing you previously didn't like. It won't be long before you actually do look forward to doing the thing that you reprogrammed yourself to enjoy.

You can easily add these "I get to" phrases to your morning Coffee Self-Talk script. In particular, it's very useful for adding good habits to your life. For example, if the example of exercise applies to you, then you could add a line in your Coffee Self-Talk that reads,

I get to exercise today! I'm so fortunate.

You could even go further and intensify the gratitude by being more specific:

"I get to exercise today! I'm blessed to have the time and energy to work out. I am fortunate to have legs to run on the treadmill, and arms to lift weights. I love making my health and body a priority. It's going to be a super workout today, and I'm so glad I get to do it."

Chapter 11

LEVEL-UP YOUR POWER BY GETTING RID OF THE NEGATIVE

While Coffee Self-Talk only takes a mere 5–10 minutes a day, there are other things I do to keep a healthy mindset all day long. Here are my tips for leveling up your power by eliminating or diffusing any negativity in your life.

Let's Talk News

I don't watch the news regularly—hardly ever, in fact. I don't feel like an uninformed idiot, either. Nowadays, most of the news is either redundant, not important, not relevant, biased opinion, or purely speculative (pro tip: ignore every headline that ends in a question mark). Some of it's not even true (Hi, Facebook!), and much of what is true is distorted to make people click, through sensationalizing or fear-mongering. Honestly, it's pretty messed up.

Yet I never seem to miss out when something actually important happens. Big headlines make it through my filter. And nichey stuff relevant to my peculiar interests comes to me via trusted curators (friends, Twitter, etc.). When something is so vital that I must know about it, I dive in to learn more. I don't live under a rock, after all.

But I tell you, when I turned off the news, the increase in my clarity, mindset, creativity, peace, and happiness skyrocketed. I was freed from SO MUCH daily distraction! You've heard the saying, "If it bleeds, it leads"? The vast majority of the news is negative *because most people are motivated by fear, and they literally can't resist clicking and watching.*

Well, not me. I don't make space for that crap in my life. I'm too protective of my uplifted state. I'm fierce about manifesting my Happy Sexy Millionaire life, and I'll be damned if I'm going to delay that happening even one day because a celebrity got caught doing something embarrassing, or a politician said something stupid. Call me when war breaks out or we discover alien life, ya know?

Social Media Drama

I now take the same strict, no-bullshit approach with my social media feeds, as well. I once wasted far too much time on social media. When I realized these platforms were manipulating me, putting me into a constant mode of dopamine-drip, addicted consumption ("gamified," in tech speak), I said, *aww hell no*. I made major changes.

For starters, I didn't like all the smack-talk on Twitter, so I immediately stopped following *anyone* who was more often negative than positive. It didn't matter if we were friends or not. I will not hold my consciousness hostage to the consciousness of negative or petty people. Imagine if everyone culled their feed so ruthlessly... Twitter would quickly become a much friendlier place.

Instagram was another constant source of distress. Because of my own issues, I found too much comparison-itis going on, and that wasn't helping my uplifted state. Even seemingly inspirational accounts I followed were, at the time, only making me feel lack. Those people weren't even being negative. No, the issues stemmed from my own scarcity mindset. Sadly, this is common for many people using Instagram today (including young people, which is extra frightening). When one's self-esteem is low, getting on Instagram, where people only post their best, photo-filtered selves, it can make for a wicked cauldron of toxicity to stew in.

There is an answer for this, though. Social media can be powerful if used correctly, and detrimental if used incorrectly. Here's how I made it a more powerful force in my life, supporting my well-being:

For a long while, I simply cut off social media, cold turkey. I deleted those apps from my phone. I did this to add "strategic friction"—like shopaholics who control their impulsivity by freezing their credit cards in a block of ice in the freezer.

If I wanted to check-in or post something, I would literally need to reinstall the app, find my password, and login. Which I did, from time to time. But only if it was important enough to justify the pain-in-the-ass effort required. And then I would delete the apps again. Sounds a little nutty, I know. But this broke my addiction to likes, reposts, and followers. It was extremely successful. It allowed me to take a breath and work on myself.

While I stayed off social media, I was simultaneously working on me, and my Coffee Self-Talk was instrumental in this. It boosted my self-esteem, and my self-love work made me feel worthy and whole. As I morphed into a new person who felt strong, loving, and confident, I found I was in a better frame of mind for engaging in formerly risky behaviors like browsing Instagram.

Once I felt comfortable getting back into social media, I conducted a ruthless purge. I unfollowed anybody on any platform that gave me even an ounce of negativity. If people made inappropriate jokes or said mean things about anybody. Did I find myself alone, in a deserted social media wasteland? Not at all. Instead, I started following people who make me laugh or had generally positive things to say. I follow leaders in the self-development field, people posting beautiful pictures of animals and nature, and funny people. There are tons of them.

As a rule, I also strictly limit my time on social media—even with my newfound positive friends. There's just no denying that most time spent on social media is simply not productive. It's mind-numbing in a lot of cases, and that's not legendary living.

I want to create more than consume!

So, I get on social for only about five minutes a day, and often only every other day. I set a five-minute timer on my phone! And sometimes, I even go a week or more before popping in.

With all the time I gain not using social media, I spend it making myself and my life better. I walk, I read, I write, I play with my daughter, I meditate, I daydream, I get up and move around, I dance, and I relax—knowing that I'm not wasting a minute, because this is all time that's been reclaimed from the trash heap of social media.

Most importantly, every time I log into Instagram or Twitter, I ask myself, does this make me feel good? If not, I get the hell out of there immediately. Remember, social media can be a great servant, but it's a wicked master. How you use it is up to you.

By intentionally keeping as much negativity out of my life as I can, my spirit shines brighter. I don't want negativity firing and wiring my brain, and mindfully filtering news and social media are one of the smartest, easiest ways to do this.

These changes have done amazing things for my well-being. The more opportunities I have for positive and uplifting feelings, the better I feel, and the faster I attract the destiny I'm designing! I'm getting closer each and every day, while loving the journey at the same time. I wouldn't have it any other way.

Thriving Around Negative People & Situations

Living the *Coffee Self-Talk Life* changes you, but that doesn't mean it changes everyone around you. True, you'll respond better to people who are not drinking the Coffee Self-Talk Kool-Aid with you, but let's be honest, there are still people and situations that warrant almost-heroic, Mother-Teresa-like patience to deal with. Well, I have a protocol and training for those people and situations, to help you manage them with more ease.

To be blunt, there are going to be times when you're in the company of people who don't share your enthusiasm for amazing words and feelings. To a degree, you have some control over this. People familiar with self-talk know how important it is to surround themselves with other positive self-talkers. It enhances our energy, life experience, and it feels good. We build each other up.

Over time, you start to realize that negative people—even if you love them—just aren't your jam anymore. You're out of sync with them. You have different visions of what's possible.

For some, this means it's time to make better choices about where we spend our time. Remember, better choices lead to a better life. Being thoughtful about who you spend time with is one of the most important habits you can adopt. You must guard your mind from external sources of negative programming, just as you monitor what you're saying to yourself.

Despite our best efforts, there may still be those instances where we find ourselves around Negative Nellies. Family, for instance. Although we can reduce the time spent around negative family members, it might not be possible to avoid them completely, and honestly, we love them and don't always want to avoid them. Fortunately, there's a clever hack for that!

When I'm around people who are complaining or whining about something, I respond with "Wouldn't it be awesome if..." and I completely change the tone of the conversation. If someone complains about traffic while we're in the same car, I respond with, "Wouldn't it be amaze-balls if we had a car that could lift up and we could fly over all these other cars?" By combining fun words like *amaze-balls* and using a silly scenario, like flying cars, I lighten the mood for myself and others. It's a simple distraction, but it works.

In some situations, fun words and silliness aren't appropriate. So, for instance, if someone is venting or complaining about their boss, I first listen actively, as all good listeners do. I don't diminish or dismiss their feelings or experience. But then I shift the mood and give them an opportunity to think something better in the moment, like, "Wouldn't it be cool if you had your own company doing ___?" Or "Wouldn't it be awesome if your boss was super generous and gave you high fives for all the great work you do?" So, you want to be sensitive to the situation and respond accordingly, but that doesn't mean sitting there, stewing in their negativity with them.

I do this in my own thoughts, too. Not everything in life is rosy, but I aim to make it *as rosy as possible* with the power of my words and thoughts. For example, we were recently living in Lecce, Italy. We rented an apartment for a month while we explored the town, to see if we wanted to live there longer term. One of the apartments below us was doing renovations, and they were using paint thinner, which was really stinky every time we left our apartment and had to descend three flights of stairs, holding our breath to avoid inhaling toxic vapors.

I'm passionate about health, and I knew the paint thinner was not doing my brain or lungs any favors. But to walk down the stairs in that mode of thinking would simply stress me out more, give me bad juju, and make me experience other negative health consequences from the stress (and the paint thinner—double whammy!). And these would push my manifestations further away from me.

So, instead, when I'm in a situation where things could be better, I respond with the more uplifting thought, "Wouldn't it be awesome if our building's stairwell smelled like fresh roses?"

Or re-frame the experience. My husband, for instance, would walk calmly down the stairs, holding his breath the entire three flights, thinking to himself that he was James Bond and able to hold his breath a long time to avoid breathing in toxic gas. Life is a game, right? Better to play the game as James Bond than a freaked-out chicken-shit.

A "Magical" Feel-Better-Instantly Program

No doubt, we will sometimes find ourselves in certain situations that are less than ideal, but we can make every one of them better. Another example of how I use positive thoughts to make my life better is to immediately find something good about the situation. It's really easy once you get the hang of it, and I've programmed my mind so it's the default. You will, too.

For example, if I'm looking at a building, and there's graffiti on it, decreasing its appeal, I look for something I do like about it. Maybe the windows or the door of the building. Maybe the way the sun reflects on it. Even the graffiti itself... I'm reminded of the Paleolithic cave paintings of Lascaux, and the ancient human drive to create and leave one's mark upon the world. Whatever works for you. Anything positive will suffice, and your brain will believe you (it does that), making you feel better in an instant.

Or if it's cold, and my hands are freezing while I walk to the store, instead of whining, I immediately remind myself that experiencing cold once in a while triggers my longevity genes to express themselves. That's a great thing because I'm going to live a long time! Thank you, cold weather!

Silver Linings

It comes down to choice, too. Choosing to feel good in spite of, er, *less than ideal* conditions, is how you navigate circumstances with grace. Your power to choose is the true source of resilience. Sure, it's normal to have an occasional dip or stumble because of some situation or event in your life, but it's what you do *after* that matters. How long until you find your peace and happiness again? How long until you shift your mindset, take charge, and turn your jam back up?

It's actually easy. You just need to figure out how to look at the situation in the best light possible. There is *always* a silver lining, and our self-talk reprograms our minds to immediately seek it out. Our default mood becomes happiness and feeling expansive, no matter what's going on. This is the ultimate freedom, and it feels so good not to be afraid of anything in life.

The Gratitude Game

Feeling gratitude is the tested, tried-and-true way to boost your happiness. Expressing your appreciation of anything, in any moment, is always a great way to turn that frown upside down. It generates feelings of wholeness and love, and it's an easy way to change your thoughts to positive in an instant, getting you back on track to working on creating your legendary life.

I can always find something to think about that makes me happy. If I have to wait outside in the rain, I feel gratitude for my umbrella or coat (provided I brought them—haha). Or, I simply say, "I appreciate the rain because it helps the plants and grass grow." Making a quick and simple connection of appreciation breaks the chain of negative thoughts and creates a chain of happy thoughts. A key is keeping it simple because that will resonate and hit your core faster.

Another example: If you find yourself feeling anxious about finances, instantly shift and think about how grateful you are that your son/daughter/spouse/other is healthy. Health is a default source of gratitude I tap into regularly because I know, when I'm healthy, everything is good in my world. If you do get sick, don't focus on that, realize that "I am glad I'm not more sick," or "I'll take advantage of this time resting in bed to watch my favorite shows." (Pro-tip: comedies and laughter boost health and healing.)

One way to get really good at this game is to pick one day a week where, all day long (between work tasks requiring your focus), see how many things you can appreciate. It can be as small as appreciating your toothbrush for cleaning your teeth, or the sun shining, or your comfortable bed, or your delicious coffee. Or it can be as big as your home, your family, your job, or your awesome perseverance in taking control of your life and living it by your own design. The result of this exercise isn't only that you'll have one of your happiest days ever, but you'll also fire and wire appreciation into your brain. This is how it becomes your default mode of thinking.

I make gratitude an official part of my daily routine by adding a few lines to my Coffee Self-Talk script, in which I identify specific things that I'm grateful for.

New Self-Awareness Creates a Better Life—Today. No Matter What!

Over time, I've found that my Coffee Self-Talk has made me hyper-aware of the thoughts I'm thinking, the words I'm saying, and what I'm hearing other people say throughout the day. I've realized that guarding my thoughts fiercely will attract my Happy Sexy Millionaire life much faster.

For example, at a super basic level, I don't even use either of the following phrases:

I can't wait to _____.
or
I can't wait for _____.

Huh? That's right, I thoughtfully choose every word and phrase I use regularly, and I decided I didn't like that one. It puts a slightly *limited* taste in my mouth, so I trained myself to stop saying it. Instead, I say something a bit more amped like, "I'm excited to/for_____."

Is this a little over-the-top? Nope. I'm on a mission, and I'm setting myself up for success with every word. Every thought. Because I now know how powerful every thought and word is. If it doesn't light me up like a giant, spinning disco ball, I change it.

Sure, my friends and family thought I was pretty weird at first. But then, a funny thing happened. I am so deliberate with my words, and I use them with such passion, they can't help but question their own choices and make changes in the words they use. The seeds were planted in them.

As I repeat my positive self-talk and affirmations over time, I find it easier to apply positive self-talk to everything in my life. Once I discovered that *every thought* is an affirmation of some sort, I naturally started thinking differently—all the time. I never take any word for granted.

As a result, I've found so many instances, all throughout my day, where I could easily have taken one road and let a complaint or a negative idea form, spiral downward, and cloud my moment. It could be triggered by some bit of negativity from a stranger, someone I know, social media, or the news. It didn't have to be about me directly, but when you think *anything* negative or critical, it creates a negative feeling inside *you*, an uneasiness. Well, not on my watch. Not anymore. Negative energy from any source definitely doesn't attract my Happy Sexy Millionaire life. So, now, I choose the other path. If something unappealing comes up, I dodge and sidestep it like it's radioactive. I tap into my elevated and mighty self-talk, just waiting there for me to grab, because I'm trained to do it reflexively.

You can do that, too. Imagine not being yanked around by your necktie. Envision a life where your heart doesn't plummet into your feet from fear. Imagine... living happily, no matter what's going on around you. Do your daily Coffee Self-Talk, and implement the extra-credit strategies for thriving above and beyond. Watch your life *go epic*.

All right, all right, enough already. Let's get to these life-changing self-talk scripts I've been promising all along.

PART II

COFFEE SELF-TALK SCRIPTS

Here are 11 Coffee Self-Talk scripts to get you going on your journey to your best, most legendary life. If they resonate with you, as is, then feel free to start using them right now. Otherwise, you can edit them, or use them as a starting point to write your own scripts, with words that are more relevant or spark joy in you.

Once you start seeing all the possibilities for using Coffee Self-Talk, it can be tempting to write all of your own scripts about lots of topics! First, that's too much coffee! But seriously, here's the thing about self-talk... when you improve your attitude about any one area of your life, it seeps into other areas automatically.

If you start with, say, the script about *Wealth & Prosperity*, and you stick with it for a few weeks, you'll start to feel better in *all* areas of your life. Self-talk boosts your self-esteem, which affects all of you, not just certain aspects of your life. So feel free to focus on one script, and stick with it for a while, knowing it's increasing your well-being in every way.

That said, you naturally have total flexibility to create whatever scripts you like. I use a mishmash of them all. So you might want to grab all the statements that resonate the most from certain scripts below, combine them as you see fit, and perhaps add some statements you write yourself.

You might also wish to use different scripts on different days. I enjoy doing this. It keeps things fresh, and sometimes I want to tailor my Coffee Self-Talk to whatever's going on that day. For example, maybe it's a gym day, or a hectic day with visitors from out-of-town, or a day when I have a big podcast interview.

Your scripts will evolve over time, so don't worry about getting it perfect when you first start. The most important thing is to maintain your love for yourself because that's where all the magic truly begins. You can't go wrong if at least some of the statements support self-love.

Enjoy!

To receive a free, recorded MP3 of the Coffee Self-Talk script, *"Living a Legendary Life,"* and a printable PDF of all the following scripts, email me at:

Kristen@KristenHelmstetter.com

Please mention that you'd like the *"Coffee Self-Talk loot for dudes."*

Chapter 12

COFFEE SELF-TALK SCRIPT: LIVING A LEGENDARY LIFE

What is a legendary life? It's a life that feels expansive, epic, meaningful, and deeply satisfying. A life in which you appear to others to have the "magic touch," where things just seem to fall into place, as though you have a purpose and a destiny, and amazing synchronicities pop up around every corner. It's waking up feeling jazzed, curious, and bright. It has you living in a nearly constant state of wonder and awe, noticing more textures and brilliant colors everywhere you look. You'll be more amazed at nature and how full of bliss you feel.

The legendary life is a state of mind, and this script will help get you into that mindset. And when you take this fun and imaginative script next level by *truly feeling* awe, gratitude, and happiness while reading it, you'll attract even more power and change into your life and your future. Anyone can tap into this source of magic, and when you do, watch out, because *life gets really fun.*

Note: If you're an early riser, then this script is especially powerful if you read it as the sun comes up. Tap into the energy as the world around you comes to life, and light slowly brightens the room, adding ambiance and increasing the dreamlike feeling.

Another note: I encourage you to record your own scripts! If you'd rather hear the following script professionally recorded, with Dreaming Cooper's amazing music, email me for a free downloadable MP3 at:

Kristen@KristenHelmstetter.com

Coffee Self-Talk Script for Living a Legendary Life

I feel powerful, strong, and confident from the moment I awake.

I am legendary. I am unstoppable. I am beyond.

Bliss is around me and inside me, and I feel high on my wonderful life.

I am aligned with my goals and dreams.

I feel like the sun is shining on me everywhere I go, and it reflects a radiance brighter than anything I've known.

I am virile, strong, and handsome.

I flow through life effortlessly and gracefully, because I have an abundance of time.

I'm charged up and ready for anything, every day.

I believe in me. I just open my heart and mind, and I connect to everything good coming my way.

I'm receiving everything in the dream life I design, because I'm worthy.

My life is amazing, and exciting synchronicities happen all the time. I am on a mission and the Universe has my back.

I feel unlimited generosity and patience toward myself and others.

I'm a child of the Universe. I am open to answers as they spontaneously arise.

Bountiful new opportunities are coming to me right now.

I'm powerful and capable of doing anything I want. I go after it!

I love doing new things.

My personality shines and lights up my life and the life of others.

I have abundant opportunities all around me. I am creative and having fun with my life.

I love experimenting with new things.

Whenever I appreciate something, every time I love something and feel good about it, I'm telling the Universe, "Yes! More of this!"

I'm open to the abundant energy that's always all around me.

My needs will always be met.

I feel like I'm flying a jet through a star-bursting sky, filled with awe and wonder.

I'm strong, curious, and I love smiling.

I look at the world around me, and I feel bright-n-healthy light and energy —a world full of optimism. I spread joy. There is so much goodness all around, today and for every tomorrow.

I respect myself. I'm unique. I feel love with all my heart, moment by moment.

I'm free as an eagle, ready to take flight because my kind heart is expansive and full of peace.

I love being generous with others because it makes the world a better place.

What I am seeking also seeks ME.

I am ready to accept miracles!

My imagination runs wild, and I'm filled with creativity.

I put out high-energy frequencies day and night, and it attracts that which I desire into my legendary life.

My energy is so wonderful, that it's healing to other people as well.

I am worthy of all my heart's desires.

I am the master conductor of the amazing life I'm designing.

I feel loved deeply and daily. I'm worthy of excellence, love, and vitality. I'm whole.

I'm in awe of nature and the world around me.

I am worthy of all the love in the world.

I am so happy, so thrilled, that I feel like I'm riding through life in a rocket, blasting through space.

My life is magnificent because I make it so.

When I love... I take flight. I feel free, directed, calm, patient, rested, and relaxed. I feel smiles all around.

I am open to receive.

I'm here, now, and ready to welcome abundance into my life.

Chapter 13

COFFEE SELF-TALK SCRIPT:
CHANGE A HABIT

We are what we repeatedly do.

— WILL DURANT (ON ARISTOTLE)

Coffee Self-Talk can be used in a couple of different ways. You can use it as outlined in this book so far, to boost your self-esteem, reprogram your mind, create a new you, and attract a better life. Or you can use it for specific things, like losing weight, finding a mate, or increasing your income. The words can also be used in a broader sense of creating general awesomeness and well-being. Self-talk works for anything you'd like to change.

This includes changing bad habits. Or creating good ones. Maybe you want to stop biting your nails (breaking a bad habit). Maybe you want to meditate every day (creating a good habit). Perhaps you'd like to break one habit while starting another simultaneously. You can use your daily Coffee Self-Talk ritual to read through a general *well-being* script designed to help you live your best life. And you can tack on to the end of it a more specific, detailed script, to help you break a bad habit or start a new, good habit. It's up to you, and your approach should be flexible.

You'll want to update and tweak your Coffee Self-Talk script from time to time, perhaps once every week or two, as you get new ideas, or new situations come into your life. And of course, as you actually break bad habits and successfully implement good ones, you won't need to run those scripts anymore, so you can move on to something new. (It typically takes 3–4 weeks for a new habit to stick.)

The key thing to remember for changing a habit, whether breaking a bad one or creating a good one, is to be *very specific* with your choice of words. You want words that are precise yet simple. Use words that are familiar to you, keep most of the phrases relatively short and punchy, and again, be very specific.

Just like the best way to attain any goal is to include specific details in the goal, the same goes for breaking or creating a habit. With more details, the vision you create becomes more bright and vivid in your mind's eye. You're better able to create the imagery—to "see" the outcome, in advance—which your brain will use as a blueprint to generate the result. Our brains thrive on imagery, and we remember pictures better than anything else. Creating vivid, specific mental images of anything you want in life is the best way to get your brain consistently pulling in that direction, with everything you do. This applies to changing a habit, as well.

Make Your "Habits" Lists

Now it's time to make a list of the things you want to change in your life. Take a piece of paper and draw a vertical line to divide it down the middle. On the left side, write the habits you want to break. On the right side, list any new habits you'd like to add to your life. You may wish to limit it to no more than three items per side initially, to prevent feeling overwhelmed. You can add more later, as you successfully accomplish the habits you start with.

Write Your Compelling "Why"

Writing down your "why" is a really important part of the process. It's your reason for wanting to make the change. The different systems in your brain (such as long-term vs. short-term thinking, or analytical thinking vs. emotional) are very much like different people inhabiting your skull, each with different desires and different ways of doing things. They are constantly negotiating with each other as you make decisions throughout the day, such as when you "allow yourself" to take a break after you complete a certain amount of work.

Changing a habit requires the long-term, planning, analytical part of your brain to persuade the automatic part of your brain that this is really important. By vocalizing your "why," you're essentially convincing yourself beyond a shadow of a doubt as to why this is so important.

And when you physically write down your compelling why, it gets you more excited about the changes you're about to make. It also helps give you ideas for the Coffee Self-Talk script you'll write.

Take each of the items in your list and ask yourself *why* you want to make the change. Why is it important for you to stop eating sugar, or save money, or stop smoking, or drink less alcohol, or stop biting your nails, or stop spending so much time on reddit, or stop whining so much? You might think of reasons involving your health, or energy, or feeling better. You might think about how breaking a certain bad habit will impact your family, or your finances, or your freedom.

What are the compelling reasons for starting your new habits? Come up with at least three compelling whys for each bad habit you're going to break, and three for each good habit you're going to start.

Let's look at some specific examples for breaking bad habits and creating good habits with Coffee Self-Talk.

Get Started Using Coffee Self-Talk for Habits

Now that you have your list of things to change, and you've written down why you want to make those changes, it's time to work on your Coffee Self-Talk script for each item.

To get you started, and to give you an idea of a script that would be helpful for breaking a habit, I'm including an example of the actual script I wrote for my daughter (who was nine years old at the time) to break her habit of biting her fingernails.

Not a nail-biter yourself? No problem, let the following script serve as an example, or a template. Keep the general structure but change the specifics to match whatever habit you want to break.

There are a couple of things to keep in mind, and you'll want to make sure they're covered in your script. First, your script should illustrate and describe the behavior of a person who doesn't bite their nails. What would that person do, that the nail-biter doesn't do? And vice-versa.

Second, describe the benefits of changing the habit. List as many benefits as you can think of. Include a description of the emotional state you'll feel as a result of having broken this habit.

Third, address the thing that typically triggers your bad habit, if such a trigger exists. Offer an alternate, healthy behavior to replace the bad habit whenever the triggering event happens.

Your script should also use uplifting words to increase confidence. This serves as a reminder of the new person you want to become, the new person you *are* becoming, right now.

Sample Coffee Self-Talk Script for Breaking a Bad Habit: Biting Fingernails

I release the need to bite my fingernails today.

I am happy making healthy choices about my hands.

I no longer feel the need or desire to bite my fingernails.

I love having beautiful, clean, strong fingernails.

My hands are gorgeous, with long, beautiful fingernails.

I am strong and confident.

I make healthy choices.

I believe in me.

I feel love with all of my heart, moment by moment.

I love me, and I love my fingernails.

I am amazing, and I can do anything I want.

My nails are beautiful, and I love keeping them healthy.

Any time I feel the urge to pick or bite my nails, I instead rub a wonderful oil into my cuticles.

I don't need to bite my fingernails, and I release that behavior right now.

I have good hygiene habits and clean fingernails. I never put my fingernails into my mouth.

I am having so much fun growing my fingernails and taking care of them. They're so pretty.

I love myself right now, and I love my fingernails.

I stick with whatever I set my mind to, and I persevere.

I am worthy of having beautiful hands and fingernails.

If one of my nails breaks or snags, I lovingly care for it with nail clippers or a nail file.

I am excited to see my nails as they grow!

If I find myself picking my nails while watching TV, I'll replace the

behavior with rubbing a beautiful oil into my cuticles, which will keep my
nails pretty and healthy. Keeping a bottle of this oil next to the couch will
ensure that I do this.

As you can see, the script is fairly basic, a bit repetitive, includes inspiring phrases of love for uplifting feelings, and also includes specifics about how a person who doesn't bite their nails behaves, as well as the benefits of not biting nails. My daughter—without me even asking—made a pretty, decorated version of this script as her iPad's wallpaper, so she'd see it over and over throughout the day.

Once you've written your script, you're ready to start reading it out loud during your daily Coffee Self-Talk. Repeating your affirmations, over and over, while drinking a cup of coffee as a normal daily habit, will very quickly put the ideas into motion. Typically, within a week or two (sometimes up to three weeks), the urge to bite or pick your fingernails begins to dissolve, and eventually the habit is broken.

To speed the process, I recommend you read the script more than just during your morning coffee. Creating a routine where reading this script is the focus of your mind for 10 minutes, up to three times a day, will have a greater effect. Think of it as "breakfast, lunch, and dinner for the soul." Or, in this case, for your fingernails.

Speaking of meals, if you make reading your habit-breaking script something you do before every meal, it'll help you remember to do it.

Something almost magical happens, where you wake up one day, and you no longer have any desire to do the bad habit anymore. You're free from it. But it's *not* magic. You created your new behavior by programming it into your mind.

There are many other ways to enhance this habit-breaking/creating process. For example, I could give my daughter a ball to squeeze while she's watching Netflix, to give her hands something to do other than touching her fingernails. Or I could offer her a reward, such as taking her to the salon for a manicure when her nails reach a certain length. I could also have her wear gloves to help break the habit.

While helpful, these kinds of techniques do not *change who you are*. They do not turn you into a new person. Self-talk can. It can change your personality, and when that happens, a whole host of other things happen.

For starters, it becomes easier to create or break any habit. Also, as you transform, you'll become open to other good habits because your self-loving brain is primed for all sorts of positive change. That's one of the secrets of talking to yourself this way. By being specific about "not biting nails," and combining it with more broadly positive affirmations like "I am a good and worthy person," you're creating a level of change that goes way beyond breaking the habit of biting your nails. You're changing the whole landscape of your mind. You're becoming a person who believes in yourself. This gives you confidence to not only make narrowly focused changes of habit, but you also gain a wider perspective to see opportunities for other ways to enhance your life.

Creating a Good Habit

Above, we looked at how to break a bad habit using Coffee Self-Talk. Now, we'll look at a sample script to help you form a new, good habit. For this example, we'll pretend you want to start a new habit of meditating daily. If this goal doesn't apply to you, don't worry, the technique can be applied to any new habit.

When programming new habits, in addition to using self-talk, there are some other variables that will affect your success. Such as creating an environment that supports the new habit you desire. Or setting reminders and incentives to make it more likely that you'll continue doing the process until the habit sticks.

For example, for a meditation habit, you might want to create a groovy environment conducive to meditating. Maybe it includes a special pillow or chair, or maybe it's sitting inside your closet to ensure alone-time. Or maybe it means having special candles, a salt lamp, or rad strip of red LED lights. You might also want to let people know not to disturb you while you're meditating.

Now for your Coffee Self-Talk script. This script is what starts programming your brain—even if you haven't started meditating yet. The self-talk lays the groundwork. It creates the mindset for meditating. Adding the script to your Coffee Self-Talk for 1–3 weeks will make the new habit easier to establish, and more enjoyable.

I like to say that using Coffee Self-Talk for making good habits is a way to make them "stickier." You're way more likely to succeed when you program your mind for it, before and during the period that you're working on the habit. Using the script, even before meditation is part of your life, makes your brain and body feel like it's familiar once you actually start. Much like a basketball player visualizes making perfect free throws when he's off the court, using self-talk like this helps you visualize performing the action, making it more natural and easier when you start. Then, when you do begin meditating, keep using the daily script with your morning coffee, and it will strengthen the wiring in your brain.

Sample Coffee Self-Talk Script for Creating a Good Habit: Meditation

I am a person who likes meditation. I am super excited about everything meditation can do for me.

I take the time to meditate every day because it's important.

I am worthy of using time in my day for meditating.

I love meditating.

My mind and body feel so good meditating, that I don't like going even a day without doing it.

I meditate for 10 minutes each day, and it feels wonderful.

I am strong and confident. I like being healthy.

I'm open to the energy all around me.

I love me, and I love my self.

I look forward every day to sitting down to meditate. It's a regular part of my life and makes me feel at peace.

Meditating is helpful because it boosts my resilience and reduces stress.

I believe in me, because I am magnificent.

I am legendary. I am beyond. I am happy.

I never get frustrated while meditating. When I notice my mind wandering, I simply regain my focus. Each time this happens, my mind becomes stronger.

I am the master of my amazing life. I like doing new things.

I am thankful for taking such great care of myself.

Meditating increases my creativity, and I love what it does to my body.

I am amazing because I can do anything I want.

I appreciate me.

I enjoy taking time to meditate.

Meditating is a great way to feel super, increase my longevity, and increase my resilience.

I appreciate myself and the fact that I take time to meditate.

I stick with it and persevere.

Meditation is one of my favorite parts of my day, because it feels so good.

I have great time-management habits.

I'm worthy to receive everything in the dream life I design.

I am worthy of taking time in my day to meditate.

Meditating is so good for my mind and body.

Creating a space just for my meditation makes it easier and more enjoyable to meditate every day.

I love myself, and I love meditating.

I love being a kind person.

Meditating helps make my dreams come true because it gives me peace and calm.

As usual, feel free to edit the script and use words and phrases that spark joy for you. As you enjoy your daily coffee, read this script a few times. To increase the stickiness of the good habit, read the script at three separate times throughout the day. Reading it just before bed is extra helpful!

Don't worry if it takes up to a month for the new habit to stick. Remember the tips I covered earlier to make the changes happen faster. Consider the environment where you do your Coffee Self-Talk, add inspiring music (maybe you listen to a tranquil song that's perfect for meditation), and look at pictures that motivate you to meditate.

And most importantly, be sure to experience elevated feelings and emotions while doing your Coffee Self-Talk.

Chapter 14

COFFEE SELF-TALK SCRIPT:
FITNESS & WEIGHT LOSS

Being fit and trim is a common goal, so this is a popular self-talk topic. There are a couple of challenges many people experience that prevent them from attaining success. For starters, a lot of people who want to lose weight struggle with self-love, and this can be one of the very reasons they "hold on to weight." In a way, the weight becomes protective.

However, when your self-esteem is boosted, and your self-love soars —both results from your Coffee Self-Talk—weight can start to come off without even deliberately changing your eating or fitness habits! It's weird, but the brain has a way of making things real, especially when it comes to your body, metabolism, gene expression, immunity, and health in general.

The other way that self-talk helps is that, with a script designed like the following, it helps you transform your *personality...* into someone who *behaves* the way fit and healthy people behave. It creates *the desire* to move more, exercise, and lose undesired weight.

Have you ever noticed how the most fit people in the gym have a certain energy, intensity, or "bounce" in their step on the treadmill?

They never look bored; they look determined. They never look tired; they look like they have boundless energy. They look like they're on a mission. That's because *they are*. When you see this, you're witnessing an *attitude of fitness*. A fitness *mindset*. You might understandably think this attitude is the result of being so fit, but that's 100% backwards. These people are so fit *because* they have this attitude. Change your brain, and the body will follow suit. It has no choice.

Lastly, many people think they don't have the time or energy to exercise regularly. Well, here's another way that Coffee Self-Talk helps. It allows you to reprogram your brain to see fitness differently. The script below is an inspiring script that tunes your brain to the "I am a fit, sexy, badass" radio station. It can convert someone with "no time" into the person who *makes time* to exercise. Like it's just a natural part of your every day. It's not work; it's pleasure, and you desire it. You want it!

As Coffee Self-Talk is typically done in the morning, this script fits right into that. However, I also recommend running through this script before you exercise. Even better, anchor it to some high-energy music that makes you want to move or run.

As described in the previous chapter, there are ancillary ways to support good habit-making. But starting with self-talk ensures that you not only create a new habit, but you also become a new person who actually *likes* doing the new, good habit. This is crucial for success, because changing your mindset is required to make the habit stick, long-term.

You might consider simply reading this script for your Coffee Self-Talk (or making edits to suit you) and not doing anything else, at first. If you want to add a little more power, consider reading the script several times throughout the day and before going to bed.

After a week, check in with yourself, and gauge whether or not you're actually feeling changes take place in your head and heart. Are you starting to feel more energy? Do you naturally incline toward wanting to exercise more? And thinking up different ways to add exercise to your life? You'll probably find that, after even just a week or two of only reading your self-talk script, you're itching to add such good habits to your life because you're transforming into the kind of person who does these things!

Coffee Self-Talk Script for Fitness & Weight Loss

My body likes being fit because it feels so good.

I am the master conductor of the amazing life I'm designing.

I love me, and I love my life. I love my body, and I love moving it.

I feeeeeeeeel good!

Choosing healthy and fresh foods gives me abundant energy.

I am grateful that I care for my body. I take care of myself.

I believe in me. I am strong and athletic.

When I'm already in a state of worthiness, gratitude, and empowerment, I feel like my desires have already come true. This connects my current feelings to the ones I know are in my future, and my body believes it's already happened.

I love the feeling that a good walk or run in the outdoors does for me.

I like moving my body because it pumps my circulatory and lymph systems, and this gives me energy.

I love having a strong and fit body. YEAH! Let's do it!

Exercising gives me energy and confidence.

I stick with it, and I persevere. I'm taking control of my health!

I believe in me.

I am magnificent. I am legendary. I am a fantastic person.

I can exercise anywhere, whether it's at home, outside, or in a gym. I have unlimited options.

I'm worthy to receive everything in the dream life I design.

I am strong and confident. I'm unstoppable, and I show that anything is possible.

I love my body, and taking care of it is easy.

I am amazing, my body is sculpted, and I can do anything I want.

I am thankful for taking such great care of myself and my body.

Walking is such good exercise, and I enjoy it very much.

I love doing sprints. They make me feel on top of the world!

I like challenging myself and increasing my heart rate with exercise.

Working up a good sweat feels exhilarating. Yesssss!

I like doing new things and experimenting because it inspires me. Exploring is exciting!

Exercise can be as easy as doing a few burpees or pushups. Once I get started, I want to do more, because it feels so great, and it empowers me.

Healthy foods fuel my cells, which build healthy tissues and organs. This builds me into a much healthier me, one cell at a time!

Being strong gives me an edge in life.

I stand in my own power. My body feels tight. My body feels strong.

I have good hygiene habits, and I am healthy.

I love the feeling of exertion while I exercise, deep breaths of fresh oxygen filling my lungs, muscles working, and burning calories.

I love the way my body feels after a workout. I don't experience these feelings as fatigue or soreness, I experience them as feedback that my body is adapting, building muscle, and becoming stronger.

I'm grateful I get to exercise every day. Vigorous movement makes me feel alive!

I love choosing healthy foods because they improve my health.

The longer I'm conscious of energy, wholeness, and health, the more I draw it to me.

My body is supple like a prowling leopard.

I am the master conductor of the amazing life I'm designing.

I am sexy and desirable.

I love starting my day with a few minutes of exercise to get my circulation going. I'm ready, let's go!

Exercising is fun, and I am eager to do it every day. I make smart choices about my health.

I am a good and kind person. I feel love with all of my heart, moment by moment.

My body loves feeling strong and flexible.

When I exercise, I feel proud and happy that I take the time to do it. Thank you.

I have an overflowing amount of energy, and I buzz with it. I'm electric with it.

I'm worthy of taking time in my day to exercise. It's so good for me, and it's fun, too.

I love me. I respect myself, and the choices I make. Always.

Chapter 15

COFFEE SELF-TALK SCRIPT: HEALTH & LONGEVITY

I am passionate about health and longevity. Health is important to me because I'm always eager to have as much energy and vitality as possible. It allows me to live my life with gusto. I also want to live as long as possible, and I join Dave Asprey (podcaster, biohacker, and inventor of Bulletproof Coffee) in programming my mind to believe I will live past—get this—*180 years.*

Does that number sound absurd? Here are two reasons why it might not be completely batshit crazy.

First, the idea of living past 180 years isn't so absurd if one considers the state of medicine and technology. We've made huge strides in the past 50 years. If you extrapolate forward—and factor in exponential gains in computer power—it's not at all unreasonable to think that science could push life expectancy to 120 by the time I'm 70. And to 140 by the time I'm 90. And so on. The fact that "ending aging" has become a serious area of research over the past decade or so—and attracted a lot of funding—augurs well for this endeavor.

Regardless of the actual numbers, at some point, technology will improve faster than people age. The trick is to stay alive and healthy until that point (reaching the so-called "longevity escape velocity"), and your brain has a LOT to do with keeping you healthy, youthful, and vital.

Second, the very thought, "I'm going to live past 180 years," sets my mind and body on a different trajectory. Our brains *like receiving instructions,* and they will take whatever we say seriously—whether good or bad—and get to work making it happen. I always say, "Why not go big?" Shoot for the stars, and at a minimum, you'll land on the moon.

When I imagine living this long, I realize there's no room for illness or disease in my life. The very statement "I'm living until I'm at least 180 years old" gives me confidence, not unlike having a sense of destiny. This reduces my stress. And reducing stress actually does make you live longer!

The following script is full of gems to instruct your body for healthy living and general well-being, with an emphasis on longevity. Feel free to use the phrases that trigger feelings of self-actualizing power and resonate with you the most.

Coffee Self-Talk Script for Health & Longevity

I feel amazing and have an incredible life full of vitality and bliss.

I have so much energy, I want to run from the moment I wake. My energy is through the roof.

I love my life. I love me. I love life!

I'm excited for everything today, tomorrow, and 100 years from now.

I am living a long and healthy life because I take care of myself.

My body is electric with vitality, and I feel young. My color shines and lights up my life. I soar like an eagle.

I am calm and relaxed, which creates peace in my body, allowing it to heal and protect me.

Everything is great today, and I feel so blessed to be alive. Thank you!

I am unlimited in energy and health. It's all around me, and I feel soooo good!

I cherish my health, and I take care of myself by eating well, exercising, and maintaining a loving mindset. The energy I generate in my body keeps me young and overflowing with vitality.

I love getting enough sleep, in which my dreams process my day, and my deep sleep aids in healing and recovery.

I radiate health. I soar. I'm full of life. Bam!

I tune in to opportunities for health. I feel them all around me. My incredible energy keeps me connected to my longevity.

I believe in me. I believe in my body. I believe in my genes to keep me vibrant and healthy.

My immune system is powerful and strong because I feel happiness and gratitude every day.

I breathe easily. My body is completely healthy, and I'm going to live to be at least 180 years of age.

I am magnificent. I am legendary. I feel young.

I feel the most amazing health and wellness because I am open to receiving it.

I take care of my body, and it takes care of me. I love my body!

My health is a priority, and it feels good to take responsibility for it.

I love learning about ways to live a healthy life. I love trying and doing new things.

I have clarity, and I think clearly every day, because I'm a focused mofo with mojo!

My youthful hormones course through my veins with energy and verve.

I eat wonderful foods that nourish and build my body, mind, and soul. I enjoy my food.

My arms, legs, chest, and abdomen look great!

I am thankful for taking such great care of myself, ensuring I live a long and happy life.

I have a super body, and I love it all.

I have a powerful brain and memory. I remember everything. Words come to me easily. My recall is effortless.

I'm going to live until I'm at least 180 years. Watch me go!

My body loves to heal. I feel love with all of my heart, moment by moment.

My body loves feeling strong.

I am worthy of longevity.

There is harmony between my brain, mind, body, and my soul. I am legendary.

The energy centers in my body are aligned and lighting me up.

I feel alert, focused, amped up, and energized, today and every day.

Exercising is fun, feels amazing, and I love it. It's just one way I take care of myself and increase my energy.

I. Am. Amazing!

Chapter 16

COFFEE SELF-TALK SCRIPT: HEALING

It's scientifically proven that the body can heal by thought alone.

— DR. JOE DISPENZA

Does this script really need any other introduction than the quote above? (If you're skeptical, or unaware of the research, read *Becoming Supernatural* and *You Are the Placebo* by Dr. Joe Dispenza.) Knowing you have the power to heal already inside you right now, let's get straight to the Coffee Self-Talk, so you can instruct and allow your body to start doing it.

Coffee Self-Talk Script for Healing

My body has the power to heal itself because it's designed to do that.

I love my body, today and always.

My thoughts hold the perfect medicine.

All is well.

I am amazing, and I am lovable. I feel love with all of my heart, moment by moment.

Happiness is the ultimate medicine. Happiness is wholeness. My happiness heals me and keeps me healthy every day. Enjoyment is happiness.

I am filled with love for my body. I am uplifted.

My feelings and beliefs impact my every cell.

I turn on my healing genes with comedy and humor. I love laughing.

I live every day with an attitude of healthy, energetic well-being.

I do not think about or fear disease or aging. Instead, I focus my thoughts and energy on living my life in the most legendary ways possible.

My body knows how to heal because I direct it with my affirmative thoughts.

Wholeness is inside me and all around me.

I tune in to the frequency and energy of wholeness and gratitude. Abundance is all around me.

I have unlimited patience and generosity because I have an abundance of time.

My energy shines and lights up my life.

My cells and hormones are youthful and healthy.

I have courage and faith in myself to heal.

I take deep breaths of calmness. Oxygen fills my lungs and relaxes me.

I am worthy of healing. I am worthy to receive. I sense it. I know it. I stay aware of it all day. Positive energy activates my genetic program for healing.

I feel an ocean wave of peace wash over me right now. Woooosh.

My body is a self-healing organism. My body repairs itself when I am relaxed and happy.

I tune in to opportunities for healing, and I feel them all around me. My feelings of wholeness and love keep me connected to them.

My body loves being strong. I stand, determined and confident, in my own power.

Every time I appreciate something, every time I feel good about something, I'm telling the Universe, "More of this, please!"

I'm worthy of receiving everything in the legendary life that I design.

I'm unstoppable because I know that anything is possible.

I am whole, from head to toe.

The longer I'm conscious of this healing energy of wholeness, the more I draw healing and health to me.

I am open to my incredible healing.

I'm a child of the Universe, and the Universe fills me with healing energy and light.

When I'm in a state of worthiness, gratitude, and wholeness, I feel as though my desires have already been fulfilled. This connects my current feelings to the ones I know are coming, and my body believes it has already happened. This connection helps me manifest blissful health faster.

I'm open to the energy that's all around me.

I am a rapid healer.

I love every part of me, from my hair, to my brain, to my eyes and face, to my arms and chest, to my stomach and organs, to my legs and feet. All of me. Every day, I love me.

Love is wondrous because it heals.

My body is strong! My body perseveres!

I love being an uplifted and kind person because it feels incredible.

I believe in me. I believe in my tremendous body.

My body loves to heal, because it's designed to do that!

I am the master conductor of my healing body.

My energy is uplifted, whole, and full of love. I am healed.

I am relaxed and grateful that my body is so capable of healing.

I am fresh and vibrant.

I am whole.

I am thankful for nurturing myself.

My strength is unlimited because I am full of warm, glowing energy. It comes from within and expands outside of myself. My energy is so uplifting and high, that I heal myself with it, and I also have the power to heal others with it.

I breathe easily. My body is completely healthy, and I'm going to live past 180 years.

I am amazing.

I direct my mind that health is mine, and it's always circulating in my life, so I always have it. I am a creator.

I feel happy and grateful, right here, right now.

Chapter 17

COFFEE SELF-TALK SCRIPT: WEALTH, SUCCESS & PROSPERITY

If you follow my blog, you know that the word, "millionaire"—as in, *Happy Sexy Millionaire*—has a special meaning to me. It's partly about money, of course, but don't get caught up on that... it means *much* more. It doesn't necessarily mean having a net worth in excess of one million dollars. It means something much broader. It means having the means to live the life of your dreams, whatever those dreams may be.

It could mean a million dollars, but not necessarily. It could mean much more... five million, 10 million... or maybe just $50K. (But then, *Happy Sexy Fifty-thousandaire* doesn't sound as good, eh?) The specific number is up to you, if you have a number in mind (for net worth, annual income, monthly income, whatever). I do have my own number, for goal-setting purposes, but more importantly, for me, "millionaire" is like a code word. It's shorthand for a whole cluster of associated ideas and emotions: abundance, generosity, success, lifestyle, travel, and so on. And one idea in particular...

Freedom.

"Millionaire" is my label for the mental and emotional state I evoke when I want to feel empowered and free to do whatever I want to do in life. To go wherever I want to go, to be the sparkling, golden woman that I want to be... to attempt bold things, to dream big, to be a badass, and to generally live an *epic* life. It is this millionaire mindset that allowed me to, among other things, travel the world for a year. And then settle down, for a while, in a picturesque, medieval hilltop village in Umbria, Italy—the kind of place you thought only exists in movies.

None of this actually required a million dollars... it only required that I think big, picture my "millionaire" lifestyle, and then plan accordingly. Step by step, it all just fell into place. Because, in my mind, it was not only possible—*it was easy.*

In the following Coffee Self-Talk script, I share with you the things I say to attract my millionaire life to me. These words are powerful. If you take them seriously, and listen to them religiously, they will give you an edge, an advantage.

For extra magic—and I'm 100% serious here—this script is best said in a "power pose." For me, it's Wonder Woman. You might prefer Thor or Captain America. Your body *will* respond to your words. *It has no choice!* And if you add a little attitude, energy, and emphasis, it's even stronger. (I'm not making this up. Power poses have actually been shown to increase confidence.)

Here's an example of how to do a power pose: Hands on hips, eyes straight ahead, and have a slight, knowing smile. (You know the one, that knowing smile that shows you have the secrets, the power, and the answers all within you now.) Yes! *Power up, dude!* If you have a cape, no lie, get it out and wear it with bravado. No cape? Grab a towel or sheet and fasten it to your clothes with binder clips. Tap into your inner superhero! You *will* feel the difference. This shit is *real.*

Coffee Self-Talk Script for Wealth, Success & Prosperity

I have purpose in my life. I have unlimited potential. I'm going after what I want and deserve!

I am living my legendary life because I can. It is my birthright.

I encourage myself every day because I can do it. I am doing it!

Creativity is easy for me to tap into, and I see opportunities and solutions all around me.

I am worthy of everything I want.

I bless my computer with love, and it brings me success and prosperity.

Opportunities abound because I attract them like a magnet. My eyes are wide open for them.

I remember things easily. My recall is effortless. I have a phenomenal memory.

I am smart, reliable, and professional.

I love meeting new people and sharing ideas. I love listening to others and learning.

When people meet me, they immediately sense my relaxed confidence. I am competent, and good at what I do.

I love me. I love my life. I love life.

I am the master conductor of my amazing successful life because I'm designing it.

I believe in me.

I have a great relationship with money. It comes to me easily. Money is a tool, and I use it wisely.

I hold the key to the achievement of anything I desire, because I am capable, and I am strong.

I receive everything in my dream life I'm designing because I AM WORTHY.

Everything I touch is a success. I go from success, to success, to success.

I'm charismatic, and I love sharing with others.

My spirit soars, and I'm on top of the world because I am my own hero.

I'm smart. I'm confident. I'm unlimited.

My talents are appreciated by everyone around me.

I am empowered because I stick with it and persevere. I believe in me and my incredible abilities.

Prosperity is all around me. I am prosperous.

I tune in to opportunities. I feel them and see them all around me. My creative energy keeps me connected to them.

My income is constantly increasing. Yeah!

Money loves me! Money loves me! Money loves me!

I'm unstoppable because I know that anything is possible.

I'm ready to dive into my day with gusto, and I am having the most amazing time! I love my life!!!

I'm organized and efficient. This keeps me focused and highly effective in all that I do.

I keep my life in order.

I am worthy to receive. I sense it. I know it. I feel it. I stay aware of it all day long.

My thankful heart is always close to the riches of the Universe. I am grateful for my legendary life and my success.

I have an abundance of time to do everything I want.

I tune in to the frequency and energy of abundance and gratitude. It's all around me.

I'm worthy of new opportunities here and now.

I am always able to take care of my needs, and the needs of those who depend on me.

The longer I'm conscious of this energy of abundance, the more I draw opportunities to me.

I have freedom of creativity for my favorite passions.

My life is First-Class and luxurious.

I feel generous with my success, and I eagerly share with others. We are all one.

I am a success.

I direct my mind that wealth, health, and abundance are mine, and they're always flowing in my life, so I always have them, regardless of their form. I am a creator.

I learn anything I want easily because my brain is super-powered and healthy.

I am in the right place, at the right time, doing the right thing.

I stand strong and determined in my own power at all times.

My heart expands with strength and courage. My brain overflows with incredible ideas. My soul abounds with enthusiasm.

Money comes to me easily. The feeling of abundance produces abundance.

Wonderful new opportunities are coming to me right now.

I'm open to the successful energy all around me, and success loves me. I am open to receive all things good.

I am thankful for taking such great care of myself and persevering in my success.

Chapter 18

COFFEE SELF-TALK SCRIPT: FIND AN AWESOME MATE!

Already got an awesome mate? You can skip this chapter!

If not, read on! (Or if you know someone who's searching for an awesome mate, you might find something helpful here to pass along to him or her.)

Recall the "millionaire" mindset (Chapter 17) that I evoked to create my "millionaire lifestyle" in the beautiful region of Umbria, Italy. I used a similar process back when I was looking for a boyfriend/future husband. It was 15 years ago, and it worked. Although I didn't drink coffee while doing it, I had a routine in which I would take a bath every couple of nights, and I'd focus on the mate I wanted to attract to me, during my bath time.

Call it *Bath Self-Talk*, if you like—though, back then, I didn't know that's what I was doing. I didn't realize it was a form of self-talk, but it was. I wrote a *script* to review and ponder, and it had plenty of details describing the man I wanted to share my life with.

I wrote down a list of everything I wanted in a mate. Everything from preferring that he wear glasses (that was my way of creating an image of someone smart), to his philosophies on raising kids (I wanted to be a stay-at-home mom) and pursuing a healthy lifestyle (eating well, working out, etc.), and so on. I wrote an extremely detailed list with about 15 different requests.

Back then, my list was on paper because "smart phones" still flipped open like those gizmos in the old Star Trek series. I can still see the paper in my memory now... decorated with hearts and other flourishes you might think came from a girl in grade school. I stand by it though, the playful visuals contributed to—you guessed it—an *elevated emotional state* every time I reviewed the list.

When I think about it now, in hindsight, the process was actually more of a detailed goal or wish list. My list didn't have positive affirmations about myself, because I wasn't aware of this process back then. But the idea of having a goal, making it detailed, making a ritual every day or two to revisit it, and feeling positive emotions while reviewing it, was weirdly similar to my current, finely tuned goal-setting and review process. However, had I included positive affirmations and self-talk about myself, it would've made it even better!

Here's what I did do. While I was reading my list in the bathtub every couple of evenings, I relaxed in an environment that was supportive of my visioneering... bubble bath, dim lights, candle, soft music. By creating the right environment, I was helping my mind enter a relaxed, alpha brainwave state, which makes it easier to reprogram your brain.

As I read through my script, I felt excitement and love for my future mate. This created that magical emotional state I keep emphasizing throughout this book—the feelings that must cohere with the vision in your analytical brain, in order to make that vision real, to manifest your dream life. The combination of my relaxed state, plus the detailed manifesting script of my *dream beau*, plus the feelings of love I was experiencing as I imagined how awesome it would be to have this dream mate, and... BAM! He came into my life and ticked every damn one of my boxes.

Did the process somehow change my behavior? Did I start giving off a different vibe? Were my perceptual filters paying attention to different signals? Was the Universe playing matchmaker when it received my wish list via the ethers? I don't know. But I will say, Greg matched my dream mate list with bizarre precision. Like, statistically impossible. It felt like magic. It still does, fifteen years later.

Here's an exercise for you: Sit down and write a list of all the qualities you seek in your ideal mate. Take some time doing this. Give it a lot of thought. This is serious stuff we're dealing with... your life-mate.

Below is a Coffee Self-Talk script to help you attract that mate, the mate of your dreams. Simply take the qualities you listed in the exercise above, and add them to this script, along with any other edits you'd like to make.

Coffee Self-Talk Script for Finding an Awesome Mate

I love being a kind person because it feels so good.

I feel love with all of my heart, moment by moment.

I am worthy of being in a relationship with someone wonderful and generous.

I'm worthy of receiving the mate in the dream life I design.

The one I am seeking also seeks ME.

I am lovable. So very, very lovable.

I know that anything is possible.

I love being with me because I'm a great person.

I am open to finding the most amazing mate because I have a heart full of love to share.

The longer I'm conscious of the boundless energy of love, the more I draw opportunities for romance to me.

My mate is wonderful, generous, sexy, and loving. Just like me.

I have perfect health.

I'm handsome, fun, and happy. I wake up every day feeling joy and gratitude for my life.

Romance is all around me. I'm a magnet for love.

I tune in to opportunities for romance. I feel them all around me. My loving energy keeps me connected to them.

I feel generous with my love, and I share it with others.

I like doing new things. I love to play. My color shines and illuminates my life.

I'm worthy of the most incredible love. Cinematic love! Ridiculously, deliciously romantic love!

My days are full of joy.

Love comes to me easily because I am full of love.

My perfect mate is coming to me now because I'm ready.

All is amazing and blissful because I see and feel love all around me.

I'm attracting a new mate who will treat me wonderfully, because I treat myself wonderfully.

Amazing new opportunities to find an incredible mate are coming to me right now.

Laughing feels good, and I am excited about all of the funny things my mate and I will experience together.

My perfect-for-me mate will be funny, generous, compassionate, attractive, smart, and adventurous.

I'm so excited about the romance I feel surrounding me, and great things are happening right now.

I am magnificent, and I feel my positive energy expanding beyond me, attracting my amazing relationship.

Love. Love. Love. I love love.

My life is incredible because I love me as I am now. Loving myself wholly means I'm ready to love someone else.

Sizzling, sexy, red-hot love is coming my way!

I'm excited about all of the romantic holidays, blissful dates, and exciting adventures my love and I will share.

I am relaxed. I smile. I feel wonderful.

I am worthy of love.

Chapter 19

COFFEE SELF-TALK SCRIPT: ROMANTIC RELATIONSHIPS

Here is a script to boost the love in your romantic relationship. When life gets busy, or we expand our families with children, our relationships often receive less attention. It's why many couples try to schedule "date night" for some alone time, to focus on each other, and reconnect.

Doing your own self-talk is likely to make your partner take notice, as you become more positive and happy. In fact, members of the Coffee Self-Talk Facebook group (facebook.com/groups/coffeeselftalk) comment on how their spouses started acting more loving and affectionate after the reader started doing Coffee Self-Talk. One reader's husband even started leaving affirmations on her mirror, and little love notes by her coffee mug!

This script will help take your romance to the next level, flowing all day, keeping those juicy vibes going strong. When you use a script like this, or add a few of its lines to a general script of your own, you'll find you and your partner hugging more, kissing more, being more romantic, considerate, and patient with one another. It's like injecting that honeymoon feeling back into your relationship, but on a daily basis.

Coffee Self-Talk Script for Romantic Relationships

I love being kind to my mate because it feels so good.

I feel love with all of my heart, moment by moment, for myself and for my lover.

I am worthy of being in a relationship with someone wonderful and generous.

I give love all day long to my mate.

When my lover talks to me, I give him/her my undivided attention.

I am lovable. So very, very lovable.

My mate is lovable. So very, very lovable.

I know that anything is possible.

My partner and I trust each other, and our souls intertwine with love.

We love being with each other.

My mate and I take time to be together, relaxing, and enjoying each other's company.

Every day, when I see my partner, I smile.

Cuddles, snuggles, and trust are always there for us.

The longer I'm conscious of the dazzling energy of love, the more love my mate and I feel together.

My mate is wonderful, generous, sexy, and loving. And I am, too.

I love being healthy for me, and it makes my relationship healthier, too!

My relationship is beautiful, and I wake up every day feeling joy and gratitude for my mate.

Romance is all around me. I'm a magnet for love.

We tune in to opportunities for romance. We feel them all around us.

Our loving energy keeps us connected, even when we're apart.

I feel generous with my love, and I share it with my mate.

My partner and I love doing new things. We love to play. Our love and color shine and illuminate our lives.

I'm worthy of the most incredible love. Cinematic love! Ridiculously, deliciously romantic love!

My days are full of joy.

Love comes to us easily because we respect each other. We are partners, co-pilots, and shipmates.

My partner and I have the most amazing relationship, full of trust and love.

We are relaxed. We smile. We feel wonderful.

My partner and I are safe with each other. Our hearts know each other inside and out.

All is amazing and blissful because we see and feel love all around us.

My mate and I attract incredible opportunities to our life.

Amazing new adventures are coming our way right now!

My partner and I love laughing together because it feels good. Our life is filled with joy.

Our relationship is filled with compassion, attraction, and adventure.

I smile every single time my partner enters the room, feeling love and gratitude for this wonderful person in my life. I am blessed.

I'm so excited about the romance I feel surrounding me, and great things are happening right now.

We are magnificent, and we feel our positive energy expanding beyond us, attracting amazing experiences to us and enhancing our love even more.

Love. Love. Love. We love love!

Our life together is incredible because we love each other, and we love US.

We have sizzling, red-hot love. It's sexy and incredible!

I'm so excited about all of the romantic holidays, blissful dates, and exciting adventures we share together, now and in our future.

We are happy!

Chapter 20

COFFEE SELF-TALK SCRIPT:
BEING AN AMAZING FATHER

You might think that no good father would need to do Coffee Self-Talk about parenting because we love our kids so much. But any frazzled parent knows that sometimes we could be more attentive and available for our kids. Whether we're tired, distracted, busy, or not loving ourselves, it all affects our children.

One of the most important things you can do to increase the love you express to your children is to *love yourself first*. That's right, first. You have to love yourself first because this not only allows you to "show up" for your kids the way they deserve, but also because it teaches them, by example, *to love themselves.*

When you love yourself, you take better care of yourself. Like when the airplane depressurizes, you put on your own oxygen mask first, so that you can stay conscious and help your children. And you become the best role model possible. Our kids learn by example, and it's unrealistic to expect them to have healthy self-esteem if we don't demonstrate it in ourselves, first.

This Coffee Self-Talk script for *Being an Amazing Father* includes self-talk that reprograms your brain to increase your own self-esteem and be the absolute best dad you can be.

Note: Insert your child's (or children's) name(s) in the script for a more personal connection and stronger effect.

Coffee Self-Talk Script for Being an Amazing Father

I love being a kind person.

I am a patient, kind, inspiring dad because I take the time to actively listen to my kid(s).

I love giving my kid(s) my undivided attention because it shows them how important they are to me.

I love my life, and I'm grateful for my family.

Being a father is fun and exciting. It's an adventure that I treasure.

Fatherhood is a wonderful experience, and I love watching my kid(s) grow and blossom.

My kid(s) are lovable. I am lovable.

I have unlimited generosity and patience. I love spending time with my child(ren).

I feel love with all of my heart, moment by moment, and this spreads to my kid(s).

I tune in to opportunities to be an incredible dad. I feel these opportunities all around me. My uplifted energy keeps me attentive and connected to my child(ren).

I feel generous with my patience, and I share it with my kid(s).

I adore snuggling with my kid(s).

I like doing new things with my kid(s) because it's fun, and we all learn new things.

I have a great life, and my kid(s) love life, too.

I listen to my children, so they know they have a voice.

When my children walk into the room, I look up from what I'm doing and look into their eyes.

I'm an incredible father because I believe in myself.

Today, let me appreciate my kid(s).

I have patience and allow my child(ren) to do things in their own time.

I respond with patience, compassion, and kindness to mistakes, and doing so teaches my children about patience, compassion, and kindness toward others.

I might not have all the answers, but I actively listen to my child(ren) and give them space to share.

I like being an inspiring role model for my kid(s) because it's important for their lives.

It's exciting to love myself and know my kid(s) benefit tremendously from my own self-love.

I have a heart full of adventure, patience, and kindness ready to share with my family.

Parenthood is magical, and I'm blessed to have my child(ren). I savor the time I spend with my child(ren).

More cuddles, more quality time, more love—that's always on the menu in our home.

I wake up full of love every day, and I'm eager to share it with my family.

We are an amazing family, full of magic, love, and wonder.

I am grateful for my family and the abundance of time I have to spend with them.

Time with my family is important because it bonds us and makes us stronger.

I am love. I am kindness. I am patience. I'm a fantastic dad.

Chapter 21

COFFEE SELF-TALK FOR KIDS
(HINT: THERE'S NO COFFEE)

Kid, you'll move mountains! Today is your day! Your mountain is waiting, so get on your way!

— Dr. Seuss

When it comes to self-talk, kids are a special case because they're so impressionable. Even small changes in their programming, now, can profoundly impact the rest of their lives. As parents, it's our job to be good role models and teach them. If you're a parent, not only will you be a better father with Coffee Self-Talk, but you'll also want to share everything about it with your kids. You're the teacher, so you can take the time to specifically teach them about self-talk.

Of course, kids don't need coffee... unless it's decaf, haha. Or, you could offer them, say, sparkling water, in a special glass they only use while doing their self-talk. These kinds of details make a fun difference. The important thing is to ritualize the self-talk experience and repeat it regularly. For maximum effect, make it part of your kid's daily routine.

Take a moment and imagine a world where all children have beautiful self-esteem. A world with no bullies, where all children had supportive, positive friends. If we teach our children about self-talk, they will be self-assured and stronger-willed when it comes to resisting peer pressure. They will feel good about themselves and not compare themselves to others. They will be happier and more successful, and generosity will fill their hearts. It truly works!

Social media like Facebook and Instagram can be dangerous for kids. Even if you ignore the worst-case scenarios—predators, cyber bullying, and depression/suicide—even minor offenses can build up over time and affect children's self-esteem or encourage anti-social behavior.

We parents can't always be there, especially as our children get older. But what we can do is equip them with the tools to thrive in this modern world. We can dramatically improve our kids' lives using self-talk—today! It starts with us parents, though. We must walk the walk, and talk the talk.

I'm impassioned and excited at the prospect of how teaching self-talk to our children will change our world. Not only will we parents be living better lives ourselves, with our own self-talk, but future generations will thrive, too. Think of it as future-proofing our kids. Join me in making our lives better by loving ourselves and showing our children how to love themselves. We make a difference!

I know this is possible because I see it every day in my own life. With my own Coffee Self-Talk program, I'm positively affecting others in my life (family, friends, readers of my blog, and people on social media). My self-talk has made me a more loving, compassionate, kind person and parent. When I first started doing my Coffee Self-Talk, my daughter noticed the difference in my attitude and behavior right away. And, as somebody who spent several hours every day being homeschooled... by me... she was *very happy* with the New Me!

We all know what curious creatures kids are. We can take advantage of this innate curiosity. My daughter saw me doing my Coffee Self-

Talk, and she wanted to know all about it. Especially because I had included nice pictures in the script I read on my iPhone. She's always peering over my shoulder, seeing what I'm up to on my phone. It was a great opportunity to teach her all about self-talk—without needing to prod her to learn it.

My husband, having grown up with self-talk, already understood what I was doing and didn't need any schooling. However, he was stoked about the idea of stacking my self-talk with a daily ritual like morning coffee. He has a degree in psychology and is a huge believer in the power of ritual, and what he calls "installing" deliberate, powerful habits. Just like installing software onto your computer.

Another way to intrigue your family with self-talk is by simply doing it in front of them. Throughout the day, I say some of my self-talk out loud, while I'm doing household chores. I don't care if anyone hears me. One day, I was hanging clothes to dry, and saying out loud how much I love our life. I was saying my self-talk out loud, to myself, but I knew my daughter could hear me because she was right there, working on her iPad. I said, "We have the most amazing life, we are so blessed and fortunate. We are designing a super-cool life, and it's exciting how powerful we are to make our dreams come true."

A few minutes later, my daughter (who loves to write stories) pipes up with her own expansive manifestation and says, "I'm going to be as famous as J.K. Rowling someday! Wait, no, I'll be even *more famous!*" Oh wow, my daughter is thinking big! I squealed inside and gave myself a mental high-five. She's already expanding her mindset and learning to swing for the fence, set "big, hairy, audacious goals" (BHAGs), and *say them out loud...* all because of the example I'm setting.

The first part of getting your kids to do self-talk is to set an example and do it yourself. Tell them what you're doing, why you're doing it, and share the scripts you're using, so they can see the words and understand the process. If the kids are young, say, between ages 4–6, then you could read some of the following script to them, and have them repeat it back to you, line by line. As they get older, they might prefer to do it alone. My 10-year-old daughter prefers to do it alone, but she indulges me when I want to do it with her.

Try to establish a routine where you (or they) do this every day at the same time. It can be in the morning when you start your day, or while you tuck them in at night. Hugging and holding your child in your lap, when they're young, is a great way to bond and share some time together. Or maybe they will love it donning a cape and shield, like a superhero, while you read their self-talk to them, and they repeat it, word for word.

As they get older, they can read the self-talk themselves and get creative with creating their own scripts. One of my daughter's favorite ways to participate in this was when I gave her permission to use dry-erase markers on the bathroom mirror to write her self-talk and draw pictures alongside. She blew my mind with some of the self-talk she created all on her own. For kids of this age, say, seven and older, they might value some privacy while doing it, but it just depends on them. There's really no wrong way to do it, in the privacy of their closet or yelling from the rooftop. Either way, you can help them find a special time and place to do it. The important thing is that they do it at all, and regularly.

Note: Kids may ask about lines of self-talk being expressed as true, when they're not yet true. This is fine. Just explain that it's not lying, but rather, "we're just programming our brains the way we want them to be."

With children around the age of seven and above, explain this *in advance*, before they hear the scripts. This will help prevent skepticism and confusion about the process and your motives.

As kids get older, if they haven't been doing this their whole life, then they'll be most interested when they see how powerful self-talk has been for you. Some kids initially reject the idea, which is a pretty good sign reflecting how they're feeling about themselves. In these cases, I'd do whatever it takes to get them to follow through, because even if it feels insincere or silly to them in the beginning, those powerful words weave their way into your kid's psyche and will eventually take root.

In fact, I'm not above bribing kids to do self-talk in the beginning, while the habit is forming. For example, you could offer a reward if they agree to do it every day for 21 days straight, or make it a weekly reward. For example, maybe for every seven days, they can pick out some songs on iTunes, or a book of their choice, or a game. And older kids, with access to technology, might like adding music and pictures to their self-talk, like I've suggested for adults in Part I of this book. I know my kiddo loves stickers and anything that includes drawing, so using a journal with good ol' pen and paper can be fun.

The bottom line is that it's important to introduce self-talk to kids of any age. And the younger, the better. Whether it's simply repeating one line a few times a day, or reading a whole script, it starts the ball of positive self-esteem rolling, and you're setting your kids up for great success.

Self-Talk Script for Kids

I am worthy of love.

I like myself.

I am a great creator, and I like to explore.

Loving myself is fun.

I have fun playing, exploring, and being myself. I like me.

I have a world of opportunities out there for me. I am excited about life.

I can do anything I put my heart and mind into. It's a great feeling.

I like doing nice things for people because it feels good.

I am a nice kid, and I feel this all day long.

I am a good person.

I always consider other people's feelings before I say or do anything.

I feel love with all my heart, moment by moment.

I am my own cheerleader. Go, me, go!

I like helping others.

I like taking care of my body because it keeps me healthy and strong.

I like doing new things because it's fun.

I am worthy of love and respect.

I'm always ready to learn because I have an amazing brain, I'm tenacious, and I give it my best effort every day.

I shine and light up my life because I'm filled with energy and love.

Life is a big, fun adventure, and I'm excited to wake up every day.

I am a fun person, and I enjoy myself.

I am creative, full of ideas, and capable. I enjoy a challenge, and I power through them with all my might.

Anything is possible because I'm unstoppable. I keep on going, no matter what!

I have tons of creative ideas because I open myself up to them.

I love me. I always will.

HELPING OTHERS & CONCLUSION

Helping Others Do Coffee Self-Talk

You might not be able to change other people, but there is something you can do to inspire others to make the changes themselves. You can simply be you, robust, confident, and happy. People will gravitate to you and want to be around you more. You'll draw them in with your new-found positive energy. I'll always remember a dinner party where a couple was seated across from us, and the wife said to me, "I really like being around you. You have such a good attitude." Wow... *I beamed* after hearing that.

There's a name for this phenomenon, "emotional contagion." It means you can unconsciously tap into the emotions of other people. One way to get others feeling better is to simply inspire them by letting them observe the changes you're making. When you're feeling on top of the world, your positive energy beams from you and soaks into them.

Don't be surprised when people start asking you, "Why are you always in such a good mood?" Once they ask, they've opened the door to having the conversation. That's when you hook them. Pounce on the opportunity by sharing your story and explaining how you used Coffee Self-Talk to transform your life.

It really is all about changing yourself first. Others will witness it, and they can't help but want a piece of what you've got! Take advantage of this and share what you're doing. Tell them about your new Coffee Self-Talk routine. Lend them this book and explain how easy it is to feel so amazing. Who wouldn't want that?

Coffee Self-Talk: Conclusion

Coffee Self-Talk is an easy, five-minute, daily routine that has the power to change your life. The way you speak, think, and feel is responsible for everything in your life. Use it to your advantage and make it the BEST, most legendary life ever. Live the epic life you've always dreamed about because you are *so worth it!*

Coffee Self-Talk is one of the things I regularly do to make my every day better. Join me on my blog at KristenHelmstetter.com, where I share more about this groovy kind of stuff, and all the other fun, exciting things I'm doing to create my Happy Sexy Millionaire life.

And write to me at Kristen@KristenHelmstetter.com to tell me your story!

I look forward to hearing from you!

> *Every second you have on this planet is precious, and it's your responsibility that you're happy.*
>
> — NAVAL RAVIKANT

∾

Related Books

Here are a few more books in the Coffee Self-Talk family:

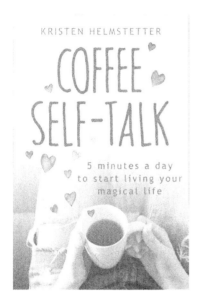

Coffee Self-Talk — *Sunday Times Bestseller* — This is the original book. It's 95% identical to *Coffee Self-Talk for Dudes*, but it's oriented toward women.

The *Coffee Self-Talk Daily Reader #1* offers short, daily reads for tips and inspiration. It does not replace your daily Coffee Self-Talk routine. Rather, it's meant to be used each day *after* you do your Coffee Self-Talk. If you do one reading per day, it will take 30 days to complete.

The *Coffee Self-Talk Blank Journal* is exactly that: a blank journal (with lines). There are no words except for a one-page intro. (I will be releasing a *Guided Journal* late 2021, with writing prompts and other fun stuff.)

This blank journal provides a place to write your own scripts, as well as journal your thoughts and progress. You could use any notebook, but readers have asked for a matching journal to make things fun and help reinforce their daily Coffee Self-Talk ritual.

Coffee Self-Talk for Teen Girls is written for girls in high school (ages 13 to 17 years old). It covers the same ideas as *Coffee Self-Talk*, and applies them to the issues that teen girls face, such as school, grades, sports, peer pressure, social media, social anxiety, beauty/body issues, and dating.

FREE AUDIO MP3 & PDF

To receive a free, recorded MP3 of the Coffee Self-Talk script, *"Living a Legendary Life,"* and a printable PDF of the scripts in this book, email me at:

Kristen@KristenHelmstetter.com

Please specify that you'd like the *"Coffee Self-Talk loot for dudes."*

~

I have a HUGE favor to ask of you.

If you could help me, I'd greatly appreciate it. I'd love it if you could leave a review for this *Coffee Self-Talk for Dudes* book on Amazon. Reviews are incredibly important for authors, and I'm extremely grateful if you could write one!

~

I'd love to hear from you and your experiences with adding Coffee Self-Talk to your life!

Email me at: Kristen@KristenHelmstetter.com

Or find me at:

instagram.com/coffeeselftalk

And come join our fun and lively group:

Facebook.com/groups/coffeeselftalk

Coffee Mugs & More

Visit CoffeeSelfTalk.com for all kinds of fun stuff to add more positive self-talk to your day:

- Coffee mugs & travel mugs
- Notebooks
- T-shirts
- And more

Readers of this book get a 10% discount (one use only). Just enter the following at checkout.

Coupon code: **CSTBOOK10%**

Printed in Great Britain
by Amazon

73929741R00112